"Adventures in Casino Security"

by

Robert Wacaster
Paul DeGeorge

Golden Paradise Security

This is a complete work of original fiction. The characters, places, situations and events came out of the author's heads. Any similarity to people, places, events or situations; living, dead, past, present or future is a coincidence. The authors had fun with this and it's meant to be taken that way.

This book is about Security; Casino Security. We certainly hope you find this book as entertaining as we found our job over the years.

Let's take a look at Casino Security and see how it all got started. It was a pretty violent trade. We used to be nothing more than paid thugs and muscle. A few scant decades ago robbing a casino would earn you a one way trip out to a hole in the desert. Who took you on this trip? Casino Security, of course! There would usually be some gangster involved, but security guys were also needed to help out. Security protected the property they worked for. If you wouldn't take your feet off a table; we would take them off for you. If you were a card cheat, we would help you to the back room and break a hand or two. We were the tough guys, the maniacs, the physical threats! My, how things have changed.

Looking at Casino Security today is completely different. If you rob a casino today it's considered a federal crime; just like robbing a post office. Who robs a post office? I've heard this comparison and it confuses me.

The word "liability" is screamed at you over and over. You are told putting your hands on a "guest" is used only as a last resort. We're constantly being threatened with lawsuits. We would be happy to sell a copy of this book to every idiot that has screamed "I'm gonna sue you!" at us. We're no longer the huge, intimidating threats we used to be.

Casinos are run by corporations and Las Vegas is now a different city. Security is a department that doesn't generate any revenue for the casino and it's treated that way. People think of us as nothing but "guards" and look at us like we're "Barney Fife" clones. The funny thing is that in some cases we aren't even THAT competent! There are a few really good officers out there. I'd like to think the two collaborating on this book are! Don't get me wrong, it's not complete paradise, especially at the "Golden Paradise," but it still has its own charm. Get ready to take a dive into the Golden Paradise.

In the book, Robert's experiences will probably be shared by a lot of people who have done this job. We have learned to embrace the chaos. Robert's interaction with Henry the Ambrosia Chef, the supervisors, and other people show just how challenging this job can be. At times he feels like the only sane person in a crazy world. Almost like Alice finding herself in Wonderland, Robert finds himself trying to enforce rules to people who think Las Vegas doesn't have any.

Though this book is a complete work of fiction, I'm quite certain security staff members from all over will probably be able to relate to this work. Please have as much fun reading it as we had writing it!

The Golden Paradise

The Golden Paradise Hotel and Casino opened to the public in May of 1997. It was another corporate endeavor to make a ton of money off a gaudy place to gamble and vacation. I started working for the place in 2002. I did get to see the place when it first opened up, however I wasn't working there from the start. It has changed quite a bit since it was first built. I know they had a few problems building the place, but I won't go into that here. There were even a few deaths during the construction and that leads to the legends of our ghosts.

The Paradise was suddenly the newest place on the Strip. Wildly popular, as all the new places always are, we still draw our fair share of the Vegas tourists. I say "we" because after working here for as long as I have I come to think of it as part mine. It was built with three pools, a "Full Service Spa" (whatever that means), and a shopping venue. We have three hotel towers and the main one has a glass elevator that can see outside. There are many problems with this elevator, as you'll soon find out.

The Paradise has two showrooms. One is called "The Jester's Court" which puts on stand up comedy. We have our own Master of Ceremonies who actually lives in the hotel. A permanent showroom is being considered for that showroom.

Since I don't get to make any decisions around here, I have no say in that for now.

The Golden Paradise has two casinos: The main casino is known to the security officers as "Paradise Valley." The Valley is the "high limit" casino and is an offshoot of the main casino. Its closer to the main hotel tower where the glass elevator is located. We don't usually have much trouble in "The Valley" since the players are there to play and win, not cause problems.

There are three restaurants in The Golden Paradise: The Paradise Café (known to security as the "Box Café" due to its box shape); The Ambrosia, which is an upscale restaurant with its own famous chef. His name is "Henry" and I personally have had several problems with him. Maybe problem is a strong word. I've had a few interactions with him, let's say. He is what the casino calls "Specialty talent," and is supposed to be handled as such. Henry appears throughout this story and I always do my best to take care of him. The third place to eat is the Impressions Buffet. It leaves impressions all right. They have a bad habit of serving things in the buffet the people in the Ambrosia wouldn't eat.

There is also a dance club called the 8 Star Club. This place is one major pain in the ass and there always seems to be some kind of trouble there. Units assigned to the main casino usually handle all problems in the club. It has so many stories by itself that I could probably write another whole book about it!

Chapter One:
Hotel day

Each week in security at the Golden Paradise a new schedule is generated.

It's posted on the bulletin board so you can see what position each officer will be

working each day. There are several units: hotel units, casino units, outside units,

and a restaurant and shop unit. We call this the "R&S" unit. This officer patrols

where the little restaurants and shops are located and takes care of any problems.

On my "Monday" (my first night back to work after my days off) I was

assigned a hotel post. Not just any hotel post, but the one I hate the most: The

Main Tower.

This is where most of the casino's "comped" guests stay. It is also the tower

with the big glass elevator that has an outside view of the hotel. Part of my time

would be spent walking the halls of the hotel and the rest of the time I would sit at

a podium in front of the elevator. The purpose of the sitting at the podium is to

make sure only hotel guests ride this elevator. It helps keep down problems if

only the guests are allowed to ride it. I hate the podium. That night I would be

starting off sitting at the podium.

I came into work in a bad mood. Before shift we would have a short "briefing" to tell us what is going on in the hotel, or to inform us of anything important we would need to be aware of for the night's work. I walked into the briefing room and sat down next to my friends Paul and Matt. They had arrived before me and waited for the chaos to begin.

Pretty soon one of the assistant managers named Walt came out of the manager's office. Walt is our "Lead Two" Assistant Manager and was giving tonight's briefing. He started out by saying "Good Morning, everyone!" Most of the officers just stared back at him. "Well," he smiled, "We're all in such a good mood tonight!"

I thought to myself, *on with the fun!*

Walt began to leaf through several papers he had brought out with him from the office. "To start off, we have a missing juvenile from Indiana to keep a look out for…."

I looked over at Paul and Matt and asked, "Is this Indiana?" Walt ignored me and continued. "We also have an individual the F.B.I. would like us to keep a look out for." He held up a piece of paper with an extremely blurry photo of a human shaped blob on it.

"Oh my God!" I screamed, "It's you, Walt! Someone call the F.B.I.!" The briefing room erupted in laughter.

"Yeah, yeah. They send us these things to keep us informed you know!" Walt said scowling at me.

"That picture is what they call *informed*, huh?" I smiled as I put up both of my hands making the gesture for quotations. "Maybe it's better to be uninformed with clear pictures?"

Walt tried to ignore me and move on with the briefing: "Range practice for this month is coming up. Remember, it's almost time to qualify with our weapons again! If you'd like the range practice time, please see Paul."

"No, don't see Paul," Paul piped up in his worst Pacino imitation, "Because I don't know nuttin' about no stinkin' practice."

"You are the officer in charge of the weapons, correct?" Walt looked at him.

"No, I am charged with just trying to help you poor morons shoot better. No one has said anything to me about any kind of practice. You can't just schedule things like that and not consult with me." Paul quipped nastily.

"I'm just reading what the memo says." Walt scowled. "You need to get with the training director and find out what's going on!"

"Nope," Paul replied, "The training director needs to get with ME if he wants to schedule things. I carry a blue I.D. card so I don't have to take orders anymore!"

I glanced at Paul. "A blue I.D.? What the hell is that and why don't I have one?"

Paul just stated plainly, "Retired NAVY!! Retire someday and maybe you'll get one."

"Hey, I did my four years! Shouldn't I get a purple I.D. or something? You're discriminating against me because I didn't serve as long as you did!"
"Maybe I am," Paul smiled, "What are you gonna do about it?"

"HEY, HEY, HEY!" Walt interrupted, "I'm trying to give a briefing here!"

"You should probably try harder." I commented, "Because this one seems to be quite out of control."

"This is for your benefit, people! You need to start paying attention!" he screamed, "This is not some kind of recess time!"

I decided not to push things and stopped talking. I sat up straight and looked Walt in the eyes.

"That's better!" Walt said, "Now pay attention because what I have to say may involve your safety out there tonight!"

I glanced over at Matt while elbowing him; "Yeah, you may get attacked by some missing kid from Indiana!"

Walt tried to ignore me again and move on with the briefing. He went on about some comedians I had never heard of performing in the Jester's Court, a *special menu* coming out for the Ambrosia restaurant, and a few other things which didn't really seem to concern security.

Finally he finished up by saying, "Let's stay safe out there!" Off we went to relieve the other officers.

I made my way over towards the glass elevator and the podium where I would start out my shift. I arrived to find a the other officer looking extremely worn out.

"How's it going?" I asked smiling.

"Please say you're here to relieve me!" he scowled, "What a long fucking day!" He almost ran away from the podium when I shook my head yes. *Bummer*, I thought to myself. It looked like it was going to be a long night.

The first hour and a half at the podium went pretty well. Hotel guests came and went. Most of them were friendly, showing me their room keys when I asked to see them. But then came that kind of person who makes working the podium a pain in the butt: The non-hotel guest wanting to ride the glass elevator.

"Heeeey Dude!" he slurred at me, "My girlfriend and I want to ride the elevator that sees outside!" I could tell immediately that both he and his girlfriend were pretty drunk.

"May I please see your room key?" I asked politely.

"Dude," he stammered, "We aren't staying here, but I told her we could ride anyway."

I scowled at him, hoping a nasty look might make him go away. "I'm sorry, but you have to be a hotel guest to ride in this elevator."

"Duuuuuude!" he slurred away, "How about if I sweeten the pot a bit!" He held out a dollar bill to me. I kept on scowling.

"I'm sorry, but as I told you, you can't go up unless you're staying in this tower!"

He now decided to try the nasty approach: "You're a dick, Dude! You're just a nobody rent-a-cop who thinks he can do anything to anybody! You think because you stand in front of some elevator it makes you a big shot, huh?"

Ok, I'd had enough. I pushed the button on my radio; "220 to Control," (At the Golden Paradise the inside officers used our badge numbers as call signs. The outside officers used their bike numbers. Each badge given out had its own number and so did each bike. That's how we identified each other over the radio usually).

"Go ahead 220." The dispatcher replied.

"Can you send me someone to help this non-hotel guest to the door?" I said staring at the two people in front of me.

"Affirm. Control to 125." replied dispatch.

The drunk and his girlfriend began to move away. Usually just the threat of backup would scare most people off. "You're Nobody, Dude!" The guy screamed and gave me the finger as he and the girl walked away, "Nobody!"

"Yes," I smiled, "You're number one, too! Goodbye! Make sure to catch the show in Jester's Court on the way out!" I waved as they departed.

Twenty minutes later 125 arrived. His name was Stewart. "Yeeaaaaaah," he droned on to me, "What did you need over here?"

I glared at Stewart, "Twenty minutes ago I needed some backup." He seemed confused.

"Yeah, that's why I'm here. What do you need?" Stewart asked.

"I needed backup twenty minutes ago!" I screamed back at him! "Go away and pretend you actually listen to your radio!"

"You aren't very friendly." He said as he walked away.

I hated the podium. My relief from the hotel finally arrived. Since it was the beginning of the shift I only had to sit there for an hour at a time before I would switch out and patrol the hotel. My relief was ten minutes late. That just made my mood fouler. I would remember his being tardy and would take it out on him later in the week when it was my turn to be dispatcher. Meanwhile, off to patrol the hotel.

Hotel patrol consisted of walking around the entire floor finding little sensors. These sensors were at the end of each hallway in the stairwell. Once you found one, you would swipe your employee I.D. across the sensor and record of this would be entered on a central computer. You would repeat this for each floor until your patrol time was up.

After working at the podium I was ready for some peace and quiet in the hallways. I decided to start my patrol on the top floor.

I was lucky enough to be taking the glass elevator up without any hotel guests riding along with me. I was admiring the view when dispatch called me:

"Control to 220."

"220 go ahead." I answered expecting a simple call. Maybe a noise complaint or a guest locked out of their room somewhere.

"Proceed to room 4103 for missing property." Dispatch said.
That would be room number three on the forty-first floor. The tower had 52 floors and now I wouldn't be going to the top. So much for my quiet time. I pushed button 41 and enjoyed the rest of the ride. I got off the elevator on the 41st floor and stopped by a utility room to pick up some paperwork. We call them "voluntary statements." I also picked up a card we call "Resolution cards." They have a toll free number the guest can call after a few days to find out the status of the report I had written. I headed to room 4103 and knocked.

As the hotel door opened, I wasn't surprised to see a young man so drunk he almost couldn't stand up.

"Hi," I began, "I understand you're missing something?"

He looked back drunkenly and I could see two other guys in the room on the beds. All of them looked pretty drunk. "Dude, someone stole my socks!" the guy at the door slurred out at me.

"Someone stole your socks?" I repeated, shocked.

The two other guys in the room began laughing. "You need to check the cameras and see if they took anything else!"

"Just a minute," I stopped him, "Let's go back to the socks. You say someone stole them? Did you see someone take your socks?"

"No," he yelled, "But I had socks before I went out, and now I don't see any socks, do you?"

I looked down at his feet and noticed he was wearing socks. "I see socks right there on your feet."

"Don't try to get smart with me!" he yelled, "Check the cameras and then you have to show me who was in my room!"

I was now getting very angry. Not at this dumb, drunk guy in front of me, but at the dispatchers. They had to have known what I was walking into and didn't bother to warn me.

"And what cameras would you like me to check?" I asked.

"The cameras in this room!" he yelled back.

"Ok," I agreed, "Show me where they are and I'll check them."

"The cameras, the cameras!" he continued to scream drunkenly.

I tried to ignore him and held out the voluntary statement. "Fill this out for me and I'll see what I can do."

He snatched the paper out of my hand, wadded it up, and threw it behind him. "Dude, you're the cop, you know where the cameras are! You need to show me now, or I'll sue your ass!"

Now my patience had finally run out. "First off, I'm not a cop. Secondly, you don't even know who I am, so good luck trying to sue me. Now I guess you aren't going to fill out the voluntary statement, so we're done! Have a nice night!" I turned and began to walk down the hall toward the elevator.

"I've seen C.S.I.!" he screamed after me, "You have to do whatever I say! I'm calling the manager, and I'm suing you!"
I kept walking to the elevator ignoring him thinking about all the profanity I was going to use on the dispatchers when I could get to a phone.

"220 to control." I said nicely into my radio.

"Go ahead, 220." Dispatch replied.

"I'm clear of room 4103…Stand by for a very unpleasant landline for your report information!" I growled. A landline meant telephone call. I could hear both dispatchers giggling as they acknowledged me.

Once you were assigned a report, you would give a dispatcher the information about the report and then it would be input it into a computer. You would then complete the report on a terminal somewhere else. The most common place to do a report was the Casino Security Office, or C.S.O. The C.S.O. would also be the place anyone causing trouble in the Golden Paradise would be brought, so it wasn't guaranteed to be quiet.

I took the elevator back down to the casino level and walked from the hotel into the casino. After crossing the casino I entered the C.S.O. and plunked down at the nearest desk. For a couple minutes I just sat there pouting. I didn't need to call the dispatchers. The C.S.O. phone began to ring in front of me. I let it ring ten times before I answered it.

"Professional sock investigators, Socko speaking. How may I direct your call?"

I heard almost hysterical laughing. "Is that what he was missing, socks?" It was tonight's dispatcher, Oswald. He was better known as Ozzy.

"He was drunk off his ass!" I screamed into the phone, "You couldn't have warned me? Tell me you didn't send me up there for some fucking socks!"

More laughing, I could hear his partner Joey answering another phone call. "He was too drunk," Ozzy said, "All he kept saying was he wanted Security up there for his missing stuff. I probably could have told you he was really drunk though, sorry."

"Forget it." I said, "Just put in the report.

"You aren't really going to do a report for missing socks, are you?" He asked, "What does his voluntary say?"

"He didn't fill one out," I said, "He just wadded it up and tossed it into the room. And yes, I'm doing a report, that's what you sent me up there for!"

There was silence on the phone for a minute. "Ok, I guess if you want to do it. What's his name?" Ozzy asked.

"How the hell should I know?" I spouted, "He just wanted to see the cameras! Oh, and he's going to sue me over socks. Just put the name in as whoever is registered to the room, or maybe Drunken Sock Man, I don't care. Put it in somehow and I'll do it."

A minute or two later the report was put into the computer. I typed out a quick report about an unidentified, intoxicated male who had misplaced some socks. I didn't think the supervisor would find it funny, but a report is a report. I quickly finished the report and headed back towards the tower looking again for some peace and quiet. Little did I know, I still wouldn't get it.

"Control to 220." Dispatch called just as I was about to get into the elevator again.

"220 go ahead." I answered.

"220 respond to room 3815 for a possible fight next door. Be advised, 111 is already headed up."

Oh no, I though, not 111. That would be Jack. Jack was always quick to jump into situations and sometimes made them worse. Just another security guy who thought he was a cop. I knew I had to hurry. I arrived on the 38th floor and heard screaming coming from the direction of room 15.

I hurried up the hall to find Jack pinning a guy face down on the ground screaming, "I said put your hands behind your back!"

There was no one else in the hallway, so I walked up, bent over speaking to the man on the floor and not Jack, "What the hell is going on here?"

"He assaulted me!" Jack began screamed hysterically. "Now he's going down, HE'S GOING DOWN!"

I stood there stunned, "Is this the fight, you and a guest? What the hell is the matter with you?" I said, finally addressing Jack.

"220 to Control" I called over the radio.

"Go ahead, 220" Ozzy answered.
"Get me a supervisor up here A.S.A.P.!" I looked over at Jack, "Get off him, Jack."

"He assaulted me! He's going to the C.S.O.!" Jack snarled.

I looked around and noticed guests occasionally poking their heads out of rooms watching us. I leaned down face to face with Jack, "Get a hold of yourself, get off him, and give dispatch an update as to what's going on before we get a damned guest complaint!"

Jack looked at me all red faced and furious, "You can't tell me what to do! You aren't a supervisor!"

I stepped back and just shook my head. Another minute or so passed and Walt came walking down the hall just as Jack had gotten handcuffs on the guy and stood him up.

"OK," Walt said looking at me, "What have we got here?"

"Jack decided to try and ride this guy, and now the guy is in cuffs. I'm as stunned as you, Walt." I replied.

"I don't need a smart ass answer!" Walt yelled at me, "Just tell me what's going on!"

"Fine," I said dejectedly, "I came down the hall and found Jack screaming while sitting on this guy's back. There wasn't anyone else in the hallway and Jack would only scream that the guy underneath him had assaulted him."

Walt walked away from me over to Jack and the man in handcuffs. "What happened?" he asked Jack.

The man began to scream drunkenly at Walt, "He pushhhhed me into a fucking wall….and pushed me into a wall, and then he hit me in the head!"

Jack began to string together a story about how he had found the man knocking on a door. When he had asked the man for ID, the man supposedly attacked him. I knew how Jack was and didn't believe it had happened quite that way.

Walt instructed us to take the man to the C.S.O., so off we went. In the elevator Jack looked over at me, "You should have helped me with this guy! This could have turned out much worse!"

I glanced over at him, "Yeah, you could have chipped a nail or something. Maybe he'll sue you over socks."

Jack looked at me confused. Nothing else was said until we reached the C.S.O. Jack kept a hold of the guy's arm as we walked through the casino. I walked a bit behind them. Walt walked in front and was the first to reach the C.S.O.

"Make it hot." Walt said into his radio. This was dispatch's cue to start a video recorder to record everything that went on inside. We entered the C.S.O.

and Jack instructed the man to spread his legs so he could be checked for weapons.

"You pushed me into a wall!" The guy complained, "I don't want to be shoved into no wall again!"

Jack again demanded the man spread his legs. I looked up directly into where the C.S.O. camera was and did a quick "Elvis" pose as I screamed "Thank you! Thank you very much Las Vegas, and good night!" I then turned and open the door to go back to my hotel patrol.

"Just a minute," Walt said, "I'll need you to fill out a voluntary about what happened up there."

"I told you, Walt," I said, "All I saw was Jack sitting on this guy's back. My voluntary would say Jack was trying to use him as a pony. Still need it?"

Walt gave me a dirty look. "Fine, go back to patrol!"

I opened the door and walked out into the casino wondering how this would turn out. They would probably try to protect Jack. I didn't really care; it was just another night in Paradise.

"Control to 220, are you clear?" Ozzy asked over the radio.

Phooey. I should have known the dispatchers had been watching the camera in the C.S.O. and would know I had walked out. "Yes Control, I'm clear. What now?"

"Possible domestic next to 14218." Ozzy said.

This wasn't in my tower. It was in a different part of the hotel. I reminded myself to start screwing around more often so they would stop sending me on important calls. I heard them send another officer, but didn't pay attention to who it was.

I arrived near 14218 and saw the door to 14219 open and then slam back shut. I could hear a bunch of screaming inside, but couldn't make out what it was.

"220 to Control, it's coming from 14219, who's my back up here?"

"Uhhh…that would be 268." Ozzy replied.

Lovely, I thought. 268 was a short, chunky girl named Shirly. She poked her head out of a stairwell down the hall and looked at me. I glared at her and started knocking on 14219. More screaming, but no one opened the door. My patience was running out again, this wasn't turning out to be the nice, peaceful night I had wanted it to be. "Get over here, Shirly!" I screamed toward the stairwell, "We're entering the room!"

"220 to Control, no answer to my knock but lots of screaming. Show me entering the room!" I said into the radio.

I grabbed the card key hanging on my belt and unlocked the door. I opened the door and saw a young, blonde girl sitting on top of a struggling man. He kept screaming the word, "No! No! No! No!"

For a moment I was stunned by the whole scene and just stood there. Finally after hearing Shirly creep up behind me I yelled, "What the hell is going on in here!"

The girl looked up at me and said, "He won't fuck me! Make him sleep with me, or don't let him leave the room!"

This was new. She was a fairly pretty girl. This was like some kind of bizarre dream, and I almost didn't know what to say to her. I tried moving my mouth, but nothing came out. I was usually pretty good at handling difficult situations, but this one really had me stunned!

Finally, all I could get out was, "…What?"

"Help me, get her off me!" the guy underneath her screamed, "I just want to leave!"

"No!" The girl screamed back at him, "You can't leave until we screw!" She looked back up at me and pleaded again, "Please, won't you make him sleep with me?"

I tried to get some sense back into my head and figure out how to handle this. "Ok, first get off him."

"He'll run away!" she yelled.

"Who are you, Daisy Mae?" I yelled back, "This isn't Dogpatch, so get off Lil' Abner, OK?"

The girl gave me a confused look. I realized she must be in her early 20's and probably had absolutely no idea what or whom I was talking about.

She looked at me for a minute and then got up off the guy. I directed her to go out into the hall and talk with Shirly. I told Shirly to get the girl's ID. As the girl

walked out the door past me I heard Shirly ask her, "So your name is Daisy

Mae?"

I just shook my head and helped the man up off the floor. He looked so young.

Great, another 20 something.

"Now," I asked him, "Can you calm down and tell me what the hell is going

on here? Is this your room?"

The poor guy was near tears as he nodded his head. "That's my girlfriend,

Saucy. We came here and I wanted to go to a club. She didn't want me to

because she thought I'd sleep with another girl."

I was once again stunned. Not by what this kid was telling me, but by the fact

that someone had actually named their daughter Saucy. "Why was she sitting on

you screaming about having sex?" I asked.

"She says if we have sex and she gets pregnant I have to marry her. I don't'

want to!" he said with tears welling up in his eyes.

The old saying seemed to be true; *Somewhere, a village was missing an idiot.*

"So she won't let you leave the room until you sleep with her?" I asked.

He nodded. "So just fuck her and leave!" I screamed! "What the hell is the

problem? If you don't want to marry her, don't marry her!" I stopped myself,

closed my eyes, and took a deep breath.

"Look, I'm sorry about that," I said, "If you don't want to sleep with her, then don't sleep with her. It's really none of my business. But I can't have all this

screaming up here. There are other people in the rooms nearby. I need it to be

quiet, ok?" As an after thought I added, "Would you like to press charges against
her for sexual assault?" He shook his head.

"Maybe you'd like to sue her over some socks? Have you seen C.S.I?" I said

quietly to myself.

I walked out into the hall where Shirly and the blonde girl were speaking. "Is

everything OK out here?" I asked.

Shirly looked at me and said, "She doesn't want him to leave the room."

"Yeah," I said, "And some of the Elves don't want to work for Santa

anymore." I looked at the blonde. "If he wants to leave, you have no right to stop

him. The noise here needs to stop, if I have to come back up here again,

someone's going to be explaining things to the police and I'll be evicting you

from the hotel; Ok?"

"But….." the blonde started.

"I don't want to hear it." I cut her off. She looked near tears and I felt a twinge

of guilt.

"Look," I said trying to be nice, "You're a great looking young lady. If he isn't

faithful to you, he doesn't deserve you."

"You're too old to understand." She replied.

Lovely, I thought to myself. The night was just getting better and better. "I'll be quiet." She said as she walked slowly back inside the room. I let out a big

sigh and hoped once again for some peace. As we walked away from the room,

Shirly looked up at me and said, "I think her name was Saucy, not Daisy Mae."
    "It's Saucy Daisy Mae." I said absently. I looked at my watch and saw it was

time for lunch.

"220 to Control, 14219 is code 4 (code 4 meant everything was fine and ok)

for now. I've given them a warning about the noise, no damage to the room and

no injuries. If you're through bothering me for now can I take my lunch?"

"You've got five minutes left before lunch time, how about you swipe your

card on a floor before you come down?" Ozzy answered.

"How about I come down where you are and swipe my card?" I replied.

I could hear Ozzy chuckling as he cleared me for lunch. One nice thing about

working at a Las Vegas casino was that each place had a dining area for the

employees and they would feed you for free. I headed down to the employee

dining room (E.D.R.) and hoped they had something edible to eat.

I entered the E.D.R. and got myself a plate and tray. It is set up like a nice,

little buffet and I looked over what had been put out. I finally settled on some

pork chops and mashed potatoes. I sat down at a table and began to eat. Paul

who was usually an outside unit walked his bike over to where I was eating.

"So…." He said looking at me, "What happened in the halls up there?"

"Jack thinks the tourists are here to ride." I replied while I continued to eat.

Paul laughed at this. "He was really riding a guy?"

"I guess so, I got up there and saw him sitting on the guy's back. That tells me he was trying to ride the guy. The guy was really drunk so I don't think it was much of a ride."

"This shit is great!" Paul continued to laugh, "Someone really should write a book about this!"

"Maybe someday" I replied, "But nobody would believe what really goes on here. It's all like some bizarre fiction. So how's the outside world? Getting lots of sleep in the shrubs?"

"You know how it is," he replied, "I came in to hear the Jack story, you know how I love those!"

"I don't know what happened after we took him to the C.S.O., I didn't want to stick around and be a part of his assault. I'll have to read the report later on in the week when I'm in dispatch. I love Jack's voluntaries, they always say he was assaulted by somebody."

"Who's out there with you in dispatch this week?" Paul asked.

"Well, obviously you know it's not you. I didn't check, but I'm guessing its Joey again. He'll want to be on the computer while I work the radio. I guess everybody has their talents."

Paul waved goodbye and rode off back to his outside patrols. I finished my lunch and relaxed for the remainder of my lunch and headed back to the hotel.

After lunch it was once again time to sit at the podium in front of the elevators. As I walked over, the officer sitting there didn't bother to get up. He looked at me and said, "Hey, I'm really tired. How about you patrol for me and I'll sit here at the podium for you?"

"You want me to walk around while you sit here and relax?" I asked.

"Well, there are always annoying people here and I thought I'd be a good guy and give you the easy part of the job." He tried.

"Walking around is the easy part, huh?" I scowled back at him.

He started on some other story to convince me. I ignored him and pushed the elevator button, boarded and closed the door while he was still talking. One more try to get up to 52. I actually made it this time. I got to that floor, found a house phone, and called dispatch. Joey answered who was just the one I wanted to talk to anyway.

"Hey, it's Robert." I started, "Am I down there with you Saturday night?"

"Yup." He replied, "My wife might make us something to eat. She says you're always nice to her when she calls here for me."

"She's full of shit," I replied, "You know I'm rarely nice to anybody."

Joey laughed, "Yeah, I guess you actually traded with Johnny and are actually going to patrol this hour for him? Isn't that nice?"

I sighed, "I just didn't want to hear his fat ass whine anymore. Yeah, I'll be patrolling. Leave me alone, though. You've bothered me enough for one night!"

"Yeah, that'll happen!" he laughed.

I hung up and began to walk through the quiet hallways. What fun, walking through empty hotel hallways. I began to get bored after a bit of listening to calls over the radio. Be careful what you wish for… I thought to myself. Finally an easy one came my way.

"Control to 220." Ozzy called.

"220 go ahead." I answered.

"220, noise complaint 3614, loud neighbors…possible…activity next door."

"Activity?" I asked, "You mean someone might be doing SOMETHING next door?"

"You know what I mean, please advise them." Ozzy said.

"Yeah, right." I said, "On my way to advise someone that they can't do something."

I went down to floor 36 and headed to room 14. I could hear loud moaning and grunting coming from 3615. I stood there for a minute; fascinated by the noise I was hearing. It had taken me a few minutes to get down from the upper floors and the SOMETHING was still happening. I was thinking to myself about the stamina the guests must have to be continuing this long. Such fervor and energy! Finally I couldn't wait and knocked on the door loudly while screaming "Security!"

The moaning continued on for about twenty seconds. I then heard a female voice say, "Wait, wait! There's someone at the door!" I knocked again.

The noise stopped and a young guy opened the door a crack. I could see him peeking out with one eye at me.
"Yes?" he asked.

"I'm getting a few noise complaints from the first floor." I said in my most official voice, "You need to take it down a notch, please. You're rattling dishes!"

His one eye opened up a bit wider as he looked at me with surprise. I smiled and he opened the door a bit wider and smiled shyly back.

"Hey, we didn't mean…" he began.

"No problem." I replied, "It's good exercise. I just need you to hold it down a bit. These walls are pretty thin."

"I'm really sorry, we'll hold it down. We just got married, you know how it is." He smiled back. He closed the door and I heard him yelling to his new wife, "Hey, we were rattling dishes on the first floor!" I walked away laughing to myself. I wondered if I would have to come back to this room later for warning number two.

"220 to Control." I talked into my radio.

"Go ahead, 220" Ozzy answered.

"Someone in 3615 advised to stop shaking the walls with the moans." I said sarcastically.

Walt came over the radio, "Hey! Let's keep all radio traffic professional!"

Back to my patrolling. The rest of the night was pretty quiet. I had a few guests locked out of their rooms, a few more noise complaints of people talking a bit loud in their rooms. Las Vegas can be a fun place and it's easy to get loud here. The rest of the night I had no more problems and no more reports. At the end of the shift I was glad to get out of the hotel. When I headed back down to the briefing room to clock out I ran into both Matt and Paul.

"So, how was the floor tonight?" I asked Matt.

"Well…." He began, "I'm making some progress with a couple of waitresses…."

"I asked about the casino floor, not your progress with some chick!" I interrupted him.

"The floor's the same." He gave me a dirty look.

I looked back as we clocked out and saw Jack and Walt in the back of the briefing room talking quietly. I swiped my casino ID in the time clock and on my way out the door yelled back, "Yee haw! Let's round up some tourists to ride, boys!" Paul began laughing and we headed out to our cars. What an ending to the first night of the week for us.

Day 2: R & S

The nights go so fast sometimes. It seemed like I was just at work and there I was heading back again. I hoped to myself things would be quieter than they were on my hotel day. As always, I wondered if anything interesting had occurred during the 16 hours I wasn't there. They don't always tell us about everything in briefing, but I could always ask around later. I walked in and took my usual seat next to Paul and Matt.

We chatted and joked until "Lead Three" Albert came out to do the briefing. Walt was off tonight so we had the second assistant. Albert was a fairly new supervisor and was still a bit unsure. He was a short, heavy Italian man who always seemed to like hanging out around the food court and restaurants. I was certain to run into him a few times during patrol tonight.

"Lead One" Stan would also be working tonight. Stan was the shift manager and was a retired police detective from Baltimore. Stan was a pretty serious guy but would still joke around with you once in a while. Stan was well liked and would always know what to do no matter what the situation. He listened closely to his radio so we wouldn't be able to joke around as much on the air tonight.

You could slide quite a bit by both Walt and Albert, but nothing seemed to get by Stan.

"Ok, take your seats and let's get started." Albert began as he walked to the podium. "We have a missing juvenile from Indiana and the F.B.I. would like us to keep an eye out for another person."

I looked over at Paul, "Didn't we see this show last night? Is this Indiana?"

Albert continued, "If you see this person the F.B.I. is looking for don't approach him, just call a supervisor and we'll deal with him."

I couldn't be quiet. "So if I see someone who looks like a shadow, I should call you? How about if I just see *a* shadow? Can I call you now? I think everybody in this room looks like the guy."

Stan walked out of the office, took the F.B.I. paper from Albert and looked at it for a minute. He tore it up and walked back into his office.

"Ok, I guess that takes care of that." Albert said. "Not much going on today, I'd like to keep it that way. Any questions before we go to work?"

This was too easy, "Do I still have to look for the shadow?" I asked. A loud "NO!" came from Stan's office.

"Well then," I said, "I guess it's time to go to work!"

On my way to the food court I took a walk through the casino floor to see how busy we were. The casino was pretty crowded for a Thursday night. I wondered to myself if I would end up with a bunch of reports tonight.

Just before leaving the casino I came across two guys slapping each other. One would get slapped; scream and then he would slap the other guy who would then scream. I calmly walked up to them, "Ok Gentlemen, what the hell is going on here?"

"Oh hey, Mate!" one said drunkenly, "We're from Australia and we play rugby!"

I looked him in the eyes, "I see, and is this rugby? Slapping each other and screaming?"

"Uh, no, Mate" he replied, "We were just getting all pumped up to gamble. No worries about this, ah?"

"So this isn't a fight, huh? You guys are just mates. Wonderful, well all the tourists here probably won't understand why you guys are hitting each other. Can you please stop this?"

Both guys looked at me and smiled. The one talking put out his hand for me to shake and so I did. He tried to show me his Australian toughness and squeezed down hard. I squeezed back. "No worries then, Mate." He said.

I continued to work my way to the food court and wondered what I would run into next. Could we be near a full moon? Security always seems to get busier when the full moon was near.

I walked by the Cloud 9 lounge and listened to the band playing inside. I then glanced at the bar just in time to see a very intoxicated girl fall off her bar stool and hit the ground. Her friends were laughing and bent down to help her up. I thought about walking over to see if she was ok, but figured if she had gotten that drunk, she deserved to fall off the stool. Anyway, if they called for security, the casino units could handle it. I made a mental note as I walked away to listen for units being called to Cloud 9.

I arrived at the food court and saw it was pretty busy tonight. I strolled by Ambrosia and looked inside one of the windows. It seemed pretty calm for now. I approached the hostess at the door and asked if it had been busy all day. She smiled and whispered to me as she leaned over her podium, "You can't believe the weird people we've had in here tonight!"

"Yes I can," I said as I smiled back, "How many times have you called security tonight?"

"Oh! Thankfully nothing ever got bad enough to need you guys," she rolled her eyes, "It was a lot of little things. One guy ate every bite of a 24-ounce steak and then didn't want to pay because he said it wasn't cooked right! I've had people asking if they could get their salad for half price if they didn't have any dressing on it. We had to turn away three guys because they literally weren't wearing shirts or shoes!"

"Sounds lovely." I smiled. She asked if I wanted anything to drink. I politely declined and went back to patrolling. I walked from the food court to the Golden Paradise comedy club, The Jester's Court. There was a man standing outside of the club who I didn't recognize. He was wearing a red tuxedo and was probably one of the comedians performing tonight.

A large crowd of people walked by. He looked over at me and yelled "Help me security, I was robbed by a one armed bandit!" He pointed at a lady walking by with a bright red purse: "That lady stole my red purse! Want me to describe it?" he closed his eyes, "its red! Hurry security, get my red purse back!" The people walking by the club seemed to love this.

I stood there glaring at him knowing I wasn't supposed to heckle the comedians no matter what was said to me. Finally I couldn't take it any more. "Hey you! Make sure the porters dust all those empty seats inside while you're performing. The cobwebs are starting to build up in there!"

He started off on some kind of retort, but I turned my back to him and walked away. I knew he was just doing what he could to get people to laugh and pay to see his show. Oh well, maybe the night would get better later. I was hoping he would be the hardest part of my night.

I started to walk away and got my first call of the night, a sleeper in the Ambrosia Restaurant. I strolled back over and asked the hostess where he was. Once she pointed him out to me I realized I could have easily found him myself. He was face down on top of a steak covered with ketchup. I tried tapping him on the shoulder, but got no response. I gripped his shoulder and tried shaking him. I heard a familiar voice and looked up to see Jack walking over to us. *Oh no*, I thought to myself.

I grabbed the man's shoulder with one hand and his hair with my other, now a bit frantic to get him up before Jack could get near us. I shook him really hard, but still got no response. Up walked Jack.

"What do we have here?" Jack asked.

"Oh hi Jack, its inappropriate behavior. I can't get this guy to stop kissing his steak in public!" I said sarcastically.

Jack ignored me and asked, "Is he a hotel guest?"

"I don't know Jack," I answered, "Let's ask him! Hello, Sir? Are you or your date here a hotel guest?" I lifted up the man's head by the hair as I asked this. Getting no response I looked at Jack, "Let's ask his date!" I looked down at the steak still holding the man's head up by his hair and started screaming, "EXCUSE ME, MA'AM? Are you by chance a hotel guest? We don't usually check in meat, but I'll bet they made an exception for you!" I looked up at Jack and let the man's head flop back on top of his steak with a wet splat.

Jack glared at me. "I don't think you're funny at all!"

I looked around and noticed a lot of people were now looking at us. Jack keyed up his radio and requested the paramedics.

"What the hell do you think you're doing?" I asked, "This guy is just a sleeper, let's try to get him up before you decide to roll the paramedics!"

Jack ignored me and asked dispatch where they would be coming in to the casino. I keyed my radio and requested they cancel the paramedics, as they were not yet required.

"You don't know what you're doing!" Jack screamed at me.

I stood glaring at him and started squeezing hard on the muscle in the drunken man's shoulder. He began to wiggle in my grip. Finally, after about 40 seconds of squeezing he looked up at me with his face all covered in ketchup. "Wha's…. who're you?" he groggily asked.

I looked down at the man and said, "That's Jack. He wants to call the paramedics and have them take you away. Do you want to be taken away, or would you like to just finish your steak?"

The man looked sleepily over at Jack. "I wanna eat my steak." He slurred.

"You have a nice night, Sir. And please try to stay awake for us, ok?" I smiled down at the man. "Stay out of my R&S stuff Jack!" I growled.

"Lead one to 220." Stan was calling, just great. I knew Jack would now be running down to Stan's office to cry about me.

"Go ahead, Lead One." I answered.

"Is everything all right up there? Do we need the paramedics?"

I continued to glare at Jack, "No Sir, sleeper is awake and eating his steak. No paramedics needed or requested." I turned and walked out of the Ambrosia leaving Jack standing behind. The man began to eat his steak without bothering to clean the ketchup off his face. I could feel everyone in the restaurant staring at both Jack and myself as I walked out the exit fuming. I figured this might come back to haunt me at some point, but all I could do was go on with the night.

I walked towards the casino just looking for a change of scenery and to cool down a bit. For some reason Jack always aggravated me whenever he was around. Most of it was his showing up at calls that he hadn't been dispatched. Another part was his trying to turn every call into a report.

I came back towards the high limit casino and saw Matt. I walked over still fuming.

"Hey," he said, "How's the restaurant side tonight?"

I glared at Matt; "I hate Jack and think he's only alive because it's illegal to kill him!"

Matt began to laugh. "He tried to roll the paramedics! What happened, did someone blink too hard?"

The joking helped me loosen up a bit. We were both chuckling as Jack entered the casino and walked up to me.

"I need to talk to you in private." He said quietly.

I looked at him for a minute and then said, "You don't talk *to* anybody, you only talk *at* people! Say what you need to say right here!"

He began to turn red. He turned and looked at Matt for a minute and then said, "What you did back there was uncalled for! You humiliated that guest in front of the entire restaurant!"

"Which guest?" I asked, "The steak? I'm sure she'll get over it after the drunk

has his way with her. Cows like to move on with life."

He turned a deeper shade of red, almost purplish. "Who do you think you

are?" he screamed. "You can't talk to me like that! That man could have had

alcohol poisoning! It can have lasting effects!"

I looked over at Matt and then back to Jack. "I think Jack's singing. Let's

dance!" I began to quickly sing some gibberish and dance crazily. Jack was

livid; I could see it in his eyes. He tried to say something else, but when he

opened his mouth I began dancing around wilder and sang really loudly, "Sing it,

Jack! Vegas is great, the steak was his date! Dee dee dee, do do do!"

"I'm going to Stan!" he screamed as he turned and quickly walked away.

Matt and I began to clap as he scurried away. Several people in the casino

joined in with us. "Let's hear it for Jack, Ladies and Gentleman!" I spouted,

"Next tantrum in one hour!"

"First trouble of the night?" Matt asked. "Want to call Stan before he gets

down to the office?"

"No thanks," I replied, "I'll see if I can scare up more trouble. No use in

getting yelled at until I have to."

I began heading back towards the food court with Matt by my side. He was

assigned to the casino for the night, but like me he would wander all over the property during the shift. We passed by the Ambrosia, but the man with the steak

was gone. Matt began talk to the hostess out front and I left him there not really

interested in listening to him hit on her.

"Control to 220." The radio was crackling to life again. I figured dispatch

would be sending me down to see Stan about Jack.

"Go ahead Control, where to now?" I asked, expecting to be yelled at.

"220 meet up with 723 near the main tower and train him on the Jester's

escort."

Oh no, I thought. 723 would be Hank. Hank was a good guy, but he didn't

have the sense of humor needed to do the Jester's escort. Things were going to

get ugly now. I picked up the nearest phone and called dispatch.

Joey answered. I told him to give the phone to Ozzy, the guy on the radio side

and was dispatching the calls. "What the hell are you doing sending Hank up

with me on that escort?" I asked him.

"What's the problem?" Ozzy asked, "It's just an escort. He needs to learn to

do this. We don't have enough people who know how."

"You know damned well it's more like we don't have enough people who are

willing to put up with Tom's shit!" I grumbled. "Hank isn't going to like this."

"He called us." Ozzy laughed, "He said he always hears other officers do the

escort and wanted to know why we never call him for it. He went to Stan and

asked to be trained. Stan said train him. So train him and then we can call him for it. You know what they say, *be careful what you wish for....*"

"You're an ass!" I said angrily and hung up the phone. I headed for the main tower and met up with Hank.

Hank was a pretty big guy. A self proclaimed cowboy, he loves rodeos, horses, and anything western. What he didn't like was monkey business, to put it lightly. He wasn't one for messing around much. I knew there would be plenty of messing around on this escort. I kept hearing *Hank's not going to like this,* over and over in my head.

"Howdy," Hank said when I got to the tower, "What's so special about this escort that I have to be trained?"

I sighed and thought about how best to explain this to him. "Well…what we have to do is escort Terrible Tom down to the Jester's Court for his show. He likes to screw around on the way there. We have to get him down to the court no matter what, ok?"

"What aren't you telling me about this? And why's he called Terrible Tom?" he asked suspiciously.

"Cause it's a *terrible* escort." I said to myself. "He's not easy to get down there, Hank."

"Well, we'll see about that." He said as he pushed the elevator button. Up we went to Terrible Tom's room.

When we got there, I stepped up to a small white doorbell near the door.

"Don't stand in front of the bell when you ring it, unless you want to get wet." I said. I stood to the side and pushed the button. A steam of water came from the ceiling and landed in front of the bell. Hank looked quizzically up at the ceiling. "What the hell?" He muttered.

We heard Tom yell "Come on in, I'm almost ready!" from inside the room. We went inside and saw Tom standing near a large mirror holding a huge powder puff and smiling from ear to ear.

"No matter what happens," I said quietly to Hank, "Don't lose your temper. That's what he wants."

Hank stepped forward trying to appear as friendly as possible and said, "Hello Sir, we're here to escort you to The Jester's Court for your show tonight."

"That's **FABULOUS!**" Tom screamed, "But you won't just be escorting me tonight, you also get to escort Mr. Funnybuns!" He held up a small puppet perched on his right hand.

I was stunned and didn't know what to say. Usually he would squirt you with a little water or throw confetti at you on the way to the comedy club. The puppet was new. I looked over at Hank who didn't seem to be bothered in the least. I looked back at Tom, "Mr. Funnybuns?" I asked.

"You need to get going Sir," Hank said, "The show will be starting soon and we need the Master of Ceremonies to be on time."

Tom looked at the Puppet. "I wike peanuts!" he said in a high squeaky voice,

"Would you bwing Mr. Funnybuns a peanut?" He looked at a bowl of peanuts across the room on a table and then back at Hank. Tom looked crazy, almost manic.

"There's peanuts in The Jester's Court," Hank lied, "We need to get going." Tom leaned over and pushed a button on the wall. Confetti and several balloons fell from the ceiling. "You've said the magic word!" he screamed. "You win a free dance and kiss from Mr. Funnybuns!"

He began dancing around the room. In an odd way the dance reminded me of the way I had just been dancing in front of Jack. He stopped dancing when he got near Hank. "It's time for my kiss!" he said in the high, squeaky voice again.

Hank grabbed the puppet off Tom's hand and threw it across the room. "Sir," he said calmly, "It's time for me to escort you down to the Jester's Court."

Tom looked stunned. "Do you know who I am?" he screamed, "You don't grab MY puppets!"

Hank leaned in close to Tom and glared at him. "Sir," he said calmly again, "If you aren't ready, I'll come back later. If you shove one more puppet in my face, you'll have Funnybuns in *your* funnybuns."

I didn't know what to say and all I could get out was, "Hank!"

Hank stepped back from Tom and looked him in the eyes. "Are we ready to do this escort now?"

Tom looked at the ground and nodded. I was shocked we had gotten off that easy. Tom had never seemed easy to intimidate to me. We walked out of the

room and headed for the elevators. Hank was in front of Tom. Tom suddenly

pulled a handful of confetti out of his pocket and hit Hank in the back of the head.
Hank was furious and turned around to see Tom drop his pants and moon him.

"Hank!" I screamed again! Hank took a step towards Tom.

"KISS THE FUNNYBUNS!" Tom screamed and then began to laugh like a

maniac and shake his ass.

I jumped between the two, "Hank!" I screamed again.

Hank looked at Tom and simply said, "You aren't funny, escort yourself."

Hank then turned around, got on the elevator and left us standing in the hallway.

I looked at Tom still standing next to me with his pants around his ankles.

"Well, that was pleasant. Who gets to kiss the funnybuns now?"

Tom didn't reply, he only pulled up his pants and we headed down to the

Jester's Court without any further incidents. This wasn't turning out to be a good

night or even a good week for that matter. Once again, all I could do was forge

ahead.

Shortly after finishing the Jester's Court escort Stan called me on the radio and

told me to stop by his office when I had time. I figured I might as well get this

over with and was on my way down when a panicked call came over the radio.

"Control to 191, possible heart attack in the Ambrosia!" Ozzy's voice said.

191 would be Phil, the E.M.T. He was probably on the other side of the casino

and it would take time for him to get to the restaurant, so I took the call. I ran

from The Jester's Court to the Ambrosia and could easily see who it was. There

was an older man sitting with two women at a table holding his chest. I ran over
to them and tried to do what I could until Phil arrived.

"How're you doing, Sir?" I asked. "I guess you aren't feeling too well, huh?"

He looked at me and his eyes rolled up into his head and closed. He let out

what sounded like a sigh and then stopped moving. The world around me seemed

to slow down. All the CPR training I had learned rolled through my mind. I

leaned close and put my ear to his lips, but couldn't hear or feel him breathing.

(*Shit!*) I thought. I grabbed him and moved him quickly to the floor and grabbed

my radio:

"220 to Control, he's not breathing hustle the paramedics! Starting C.P.R.!" I

said.

I pulled out the mouth guard from my belt and placed it over his mouth. I then

leaned in while holding his nose and blew two quick breaths into his mouth. I

began doing chest compressions and then gave two more breaths. During the next

round of chest compressions Phil showed up. Just as he knelt down to help me

with the C.P.R, the man suddenly threw up and started coughing. We rolled him

onto his side so he wouldn't choke on his vomit. The man opened his eyes and

looked up at me. As our eyes met I could suddenly feel my own heart beating so

loud and hard I thought it was going to burst out of my chest. I realized I was huffing and puffing.

Shortly the paramedics showed up and took over. I moved myself over to an empty table and sat down. I was still a bit jacked up from all the adrenaline in my system. Phil was talking to the two ladies who were with the man. He seemed to be getting the information for the report, as he was also writing in a small notebook. He glanced in my direction and then walked over.

Phil took a closer look at me and said, "Are you all right, Robert? You're pretty pale."

"Yeah," I responded, still feeling a bit shocked from the whole situation, "Is he going to be ok?"

Phil smiled from ear to ear. "Yeah, the paramedics said they think you saved him by doing C.P.R." I watched as they loaded the man onto a gurney. It gave me a good feeling to see the man moving and speaking to the paramedics.

"I'm fine." I said to Phil, "Get the information for your report before everybody leaves."

I looked up to see Stan standing at the restaurant entrance looking over at me. I picked up a glass sitting on the table and offered him an imaginary toast. He smiled, walked over and sat down at the table next to me.

"You did a good job saving that guy." He said.

I looked him in the eyes, "How about you yell at me now about Jack while I'm still jacked up on adrenaline and probably won't remember what you say?"

"You're one of my top officers," he said smiling, "You always do such a good job dealing with anybody and everybody in the casino, no matter what problems they cause. So why can't you get along with Jack?"

"He's an idiot!" I replied.

"That may be," he countered, "But he's still an officer like you and you really need to try and get along with him. He said you humiliated him by screaming at someone's food?"

"Oh he's a moron!" I said, "He wanted to know if the guy's steak was a hotel guest, so I asked it!"

"Please try to get along with him," Stan pleaded, "I don't need him in my office all the time complaining about you, Matt, or Paul!"

"I'll do what I can." I said, "How about you try to keep him away from places he doesn't need to be? His post was in the casino tonight and I didn't ask for back up for a sleeper. He comes for a sleeper, but this guy stops breathing after eating some bad tuna and Jack doesn't even show up."

"Bad tuna stopped his breathing?" Stan asked.

"I blame everything that happens here on bad tuna." I explained

Stan chuckled and told me not to let the French Chef hear that. He got up and mentioned again what a good job I did with the C.P.R. and then walked away.

The night clearly wasn't going well. What a pessimistic way to look at things, I guess. On the other hand, a man had stopped breathing and I saved him by doing something I always joke about in class. Maybe tonight wasn't going so bad after all? I got up and walked out of the restaurant feeling much better about the night. Dispatch decided I deserved a lunch after that so I went downstairs to the employee dining area.

I decided to get something light and made myself a small salad. I figured I deserved a treat for all my trouble so far and got myself two glasses of chocolate milk. While looking for somewhere to sit down I saw Stewart sitting at a table and sat down next to him. I hadn't seen him since last night when I was waiting for backup at the tower podium. I gave him a quick hello and started to eat my salad.

He looked up at me and said, "Hey, didn't the paramedics go to the Ambrosia a little bit ago?"

I stopped eating and just looked at him for a minute. "Yeah." I answered.

"What happened there?" he asked.

Typical Stewart wasn't listening to his radio very closely. "Bad Tuna." I answered.

"Again?" he asked, "They seem to have a lot of bad tuna there, don't they?"

"Yes they do!" I chuckled, "They certainly do serve a lot of bad tuna there."

I continued eating my salad while chuckling to myself that Stewart just accepted whatever I said. I mused to myself how lucky the choking man was that I was the officer who responded and not someone less aggressive. I could picture a few other officers shrugging when the paramedics asked them why they hadn't done C.P.R.

I finished the rest of my salad and just sat there drinking my chocolate milk. I spent most of my lunch just sipping away and finally decided that I also deserved some ice cream. Some cones were sitting out near the ice cream machine so I made myself one just as Ozzy was calling me on the radio again.

"Control to 220 at lunch."

I licked my cone a few times before answering, "Go ahead, what is it this time?"

"Can you clear your lunch a bit early? I have an employee accident in the Ambrosia kitchen and Phil's tied up doing that last report."

An accident, lovely, I thought to myself. I never liked accident reports, especially employee accidents. Too much paperwork for me to do. I walked back upstairs through the food court and over to the Ambrosia still holding and nursing my ice cream cone. When I got to the restaurant I was directed back to the kitchen. I arrived to a crowd of chefs gathered around a guy holding a bloody towel.

"How're you guys doing?" I asked as I walked up, "Looks like we have a bit of a problem here."

The chefs parted and one of the better English speakers said, "Ee cut is finger while shopping!"

I looked at him and cocked my head, "Shopping?"

The chef produced a knife and simulated a chopping motion for me. Now that I understood, I moved the chef out of the kitchen and into a back office so no food would be contaminated from the blood. I gulped down the last of my cone then had him remove the towel so I could look at his wound. The poor guy had chopped off what looked like a good part of the end of his finger. I called Ozzy and had him once again roll the paramedics. I also asked him to have another officer bring me the paperwork and a camera to document the accident. I didn't know if he was trying to be funny or what, but Ozzy dispatched Jack to bring me the supplies I asked for.

While waiting, I asked what the chef had been chopping and was told he was cutting some liver. The meat had gotten some blood on it and was now unusable. I asked if someone could bring it to me anyway. Soon I had a large piece of liver with a bit of blood on it.

Jack entered the office with the camera and paperwork and gave me a dirty look. He handed me the paperwork and camera and the smiled at the chef, "A little accident, huh?"

"It's more inappropriate activity, Jack." I answered for the chef, "He was assaulted by this liver and now wants to *press charges!*" I shoved the liver under his nose and began to scream for Jack to take it into custody! The chefs began to laugh, including the chef with the cut finger. This only encouraged me. I pulled out my handcuffs and attempted to lock them around the liver.

I suddenly yanked the liver out of the cuffs and screamed, "Run Jack, it's gotten loose!" I slapped Jack across the face with the liver and threw it on the floor. The chefs roared with laughter! Jack turned purple and for a minute I almost thought his head was going to explode.

He looked like he was about to scream something at me, or attack me, but all that came out of his mouth was a loud, "Ghuuuuu!" He turned and stomped out the door probably going right to a phone to call Stan again. I just couldn't stop picking on him. I guess I just don't work and play well with some people.

As he left I yelled, "Next meat show will be in two hours, Jack! Don't miss it!"

Jack left and the paramedics arrived on scene. I told them the situation and took a few pictures of the cut finger, the knife he had used, and even the liver. The paramedics decided the chef was cut bad enough to go with them to the hospital. I got his name and told him to go with them. I would wait to fill out all the paperwork when he returned from the emergency room. He would just need to go to the Security booth in the main casino when he got back. I wished him well and off he went.

As I was leaving, the head Chef, "Henry" *(pronounced Onry)* stopped me. "Aren't you zee same man who save the eart attack diner?"

I nodded, "Yup that was me, too. I just can't seem to stay out of here tonight."

"You should be proud." He said, "Would you like somezing to eat?"

Part of me wanted to say yes, to sit down for a nice, fat steak, or maybe some liver. Ha ha. I declined and told him I would probably be yelled at later for harassing Jack. He looked at me and said, "But zis Jack, he let zee liver get away!" He began to laugh and then asked where he could call my supervisor. I told him I would have a supervisor call the kitchen if he wanted. I notified dispatch and asked them to pass the message on to Stan. No matter what the chef said to Stan, I still expected to be yelled at later. Verbally harassing Jack was one thing, hitting him with a piece of liver was another. Oh well, all I could do was go on with the night.

I walked out of the Ambrosia and found Matt waiting for me. "What are you doing isn't there some chick for you to be hitting on in the casino?"

He smiled and ignored the comment. "C.P.R., and now an employee accident? Are we trying to take Phil's place?"

"Not at all," I replied, "I respond and harass Jack and Phil does the reports."

"I saw him run out of here," Matt smiled, "What did you do to him this time?"

"I hit him in the face with some bloody liver."

Matt started to laugh. "Come on, go outside with me while I have a smoke." I followed him out a side door into the hot night air. I really hated the summer time. We just stood there for a bit while Matt lit up a cigarette and took a deep drag.

Finally he spoke, "I don't think it's fair for you to be hitting him with meat without Paul and me there."

"I'll be working the casino next shift, how about you?" I asked.
"Yup," he replied, "I checked and it'll be me, you, Cortez and Jack."

"*Cortez?*" I asked, "Oh no. We'll never see him, he always hides! Just more work for us."

"Yeah, but I know where he hides now." Matt smiled.

"Is that so?" I chuckled, "Maybe we can hit him with some liver? I'll have to give Paul some liver for his outside post, so he can hit him, too."

Matt finished his cigarette and we walked back in the side door. "You should put all this energy into women, they're much more fun."

"To you maybe," I replied, "But I think I'll just keep working Jack." He was laughing as we parted ways.

I walked back inside and toured around near The Jester's Court again. I could hear the show going on inside and occasional laughter. I strolled past the main entrance and slipped into a back entrance. I snuck into the "Green Room." Tom was sitting on a couch next to the comedian who had been yelling at me while standing outside of the Theater.

"Well, if it isn't Mr. Security!" the comedian said, standing up, "I wasn't too hard on you out there before the show, was I?"

I shook my head, smiling, "Nah, I just couldn't let you go on without my own retort! No hard feelings." I held out my hand and the comedian shook it.

"Hey, what was the deal with the big, nasty guy on the escort?" Tom asked.

"Who, Hank?" I asked in return, "He's really ok, he just didn't know what he was walking into. He thought the escort would be easy."

"I keep telling you guys I get all hopped up before a show and you need to send people who have a sense of humor!" Tom said. To illustrate his point, he reached into his jacket pocket and tossed some confetti at me. "Wheeee!" he said quietly.

I chuckled and walked over to a small refrigerator. "You guys don't mind, do you?" I reached inside and took out a small bottle of Pepsi. I opened it and gulped it down in several large swallows.

"That belonged to Mr. Funnybuns!" Tom screamed, "I'll have to tell him now! Oh the horror, the horror!" The comedian on stage was finishing his act and we could hear applause. Tom threw one more handful of confetti at me and then walked out of the Green Room towards the stage to introduce the next comedian.

I looked at the other comedian who was now standing near the door waiting for Tom to introduce him. "Good luck," I said as I walked back out the way I had come in, "And try not to drink all of Mr. Funnybuns' Pepsi!" I could only chuckle to myself as I walked back out towards the Ambrosia.

Things seemed to have calmed down for the night. Hopefully they would stay that way. I wandered around looking in the shops and restaurants, checking out all the people. Most of the people were gathered in the fast food area. Getting

bored I strolled back towards the casino. Just as I got to the edge of the casino a

man walked up to me looking confused.

"Where are the elevators that go up? He asked

I always hate questions like that. "All the elevators here go up."

"No," he said aggravated, "Where are the ones that go UP!"

"They all go up," I said getting aggravated myself, "That's what elevators do,

they go up."

Now he tried a different type of confusion, "Ok, How can I go up?"

"Take an elevator." I said and began to walk away.

"Where are they!" the man screamed at me as I was walking away.

I waved my hand around my head in a circle and said, "All around us. Just

look for the things that go up." The man didn't follow me as I walked away. I

was glad as he was getting on my nerves. I'm sure he just wanted to go up to his

room and maybe I should have helped him. Maybe he'll run into Jack, I thought,

and Jack will show him an elevator that goes up.

I looked down at my watch and was surprised to see it was almost the end of

the shift. Time goes by fast when you're busy. I thought about the old man and

wondered how he was doing in the hospital; if the C.P.R. had really helped him.

Sometimes you never hear from someone like that again. I looked into the casino

just in time to see a man fall off his seat at a blackjack table. I stood, watched, and waited for the inevitable panic. Someone in the pit grabbed a phone and was screaming into it. Here came the panic. After a few seconds my radio blared to life: "Control to 111," Ozzy was calling Jack's number finally. I loved it. I moved over to a spot near the pit for a good vantage point of the show.

"111 go ahead!" Jack screamed back into his radio.

"Guest fell off his chair at pit 14."

"Pit 14!" Jack yelled back enthusiastically. I looked around the casino and spotted Jack on the other side almost sprinting to Pit 14. This might be pretty funny.

"Control to 187, back him up at Pit 14." Ozzy said, calling Matt.

Now they called Matt to help Jack out. I saw Matt coming from my side of the casino and as he started to pass me I put out a hand and stopped him. He looked over at me and I shook my head smiling. "Not unless he really needs you." I smiled, "Just watch the show." Matt settled back next to me and we watched Jack arrive and bend over the man.

Jack at first just stood there bent over speaking to the unconscious person. After getting no response he crouched down and shook the man. He still got no response from the man. Jack rolled the man over onto his back and leaned down to place his ear over the man's mouth to listen to breathing I guess. As he got right down close to the man's mouth the man suddenly, almost violently threw up into Jack's ear. I roared with laughter and began clapping! Jack stood up but didn't seem to know what to do now. He heard the laughing and clapping and looked over to where Matt and I were standing. He gave us both a look that I'm sure was meant to show us he was mad, but instead it just made me laugh and clap harder. I looked over at Matt who was now laughing, too. I calmed myself for a minute and then said into the radio: "Turn him over Jack, before he chokes on all that bio!"

Jack leaned back down to turn the man over, but before he could the man sat up.

I pushed my radio button again and said, "You're a miracle worker!" I then turned around and began to walk back towards the restaurants still giggling to myself.

"Aren't you going to watch the rest?" Matt asked.

"Nope," I smiled, "That's all I needed to see."

I listened to Jack spend the next half hour calling dispatch to find out if the man was a hotel guest and where he was staying. Eventually Matt brought a wheelchair over and the two of them poured the man into it. They took him up to his room and poured him into there. I'm sure Jack gave Matt dirty looks all the way up. It was finally close to quitting time, so I headed towards the briefing room to clock out. It had been one hell of a long night for me. Time for someone else to deal with the heart attacks, missing property, accidents and passed out people for a while. I was hoping to escape without having to talk to Stan, but didn't quite make it. I about to clock out and was waiting for Paul and Matt when Stan poked his head out of his office and saw me.

"You want to step in here for a minute?" He said looking at me.
"Are you sure it's me you want?" I said quietly, "I'm totally innocent no matter what people say!"

He signaled me inward with one finger and in I came. I walked in and he closed the door behind me. Stan pointed to a chair and I sat down. He sat down behind his desk and looked at me for a minute. "What am I going to do with you?" he asked.

"How about let me leave and pretend I didn't do whatever it was?" I suggested.

Stan shook his head and looked at his desk for a minute. "Did you really hit him in the face with some meat?"

"Hey," I said, "It was escaping! I tried to restrain it! Can I help it if he doesn't have a sense of humor?"

"Don't hit him with any more meat, or anything else for that matter!" Stan growled, "I told you, I don't need him in here all the time crying about what people do to him! It's either you, or Paul, or Matt! Every night I have to listen to him! I don't want this going on tomorrow night! You two are on the floor together and I expect you to GET ALONG!"

I looked around the office and said quietly, "Yeah."

"How about a little more enthusiasm?" Stan asked, "I'm quite certain you didn't hit him quietly!"

"Actually," I quipped, "It was the liver that hit him."
Stan glared at me. "Ok, ok!" I said, "You win, I'll try not to aggravate him. But you know he asks for this stuff!"

"You're a good officer," Stan said again, "Don't make me start writing you up over him, he's not worth it!"

I looked at Stan. He was going to let me slide for tonight. I didn't know whether to be happy or not. I knew Jack would probably be mad when he found out I was just given a short lecture for hitting him. Oh well, who cared what Jack thought anyway?

I stood up and held out my hand to shake Stan's. "I promise I'll be good tomorrow."

Stan shook my hand and said, "Good, that's all I ask. You did a great job tonight, so go home and get some rest. I'll see you tomorrow."

I walked out the door and noticed both Paul and Matt were waiting for me. Both were also anxious to hear what had happened in the office. I clocked out and filled them both in on the way out to our cars. I was almost looking forward to tomorrow night. My mind started working on ways to bother Jack while trying to appear pleasant at the same time. And if not Jack, there was always someone else I could heckle. Cortez would be on the floor with us; maybe I would just target him. Through all the bad things, I still liked working security.

Three: Casino and Club

I walked into the casino and looked around. Things didn't feel right. Here I was, right where I was supposed to be, but things just didn't feel right. I started heading towards the Cloud 9 Lounge. Something seemed to be wrong with the lighting because it looked as if the lounge was shaded black and white. There was usually a band playing, but this time there just seemed to be someone up there on stage that resembled Frank Sinatra. He was holding a drink, a cigarette, and singing into the microphone. Things really seemed out of place. Something brushed against me. I turned around to see a herd of cows walking past the lounge. How the hell did cows get into the casino? I tried to scream at them but nothing came out of my mouth. Finally I reached over and slapped one of the cows on the behind to get its attention. When it turned around to look at me, it had Cortez' head!

"Moo, moo, moo. Where can I take a nap?" it asked me.

I sat straight up in bed and turned to look at the alarm going off next to me. Just another weird Golden Paradise dream. Sheesh. Time to get up and go to work. I figured I just had an active imagination. I got ready and left for work.

I thought about this dream the entire drive to work. I just couldn't shake it. What did seeing Frank Sinatra and a cow with a Cortez head mean? Hopefully something would take my mind away from this strange dream. I walked into the briefing room and sat down in my usual spot.

"Hey," Paul said looking at me, "What's the deal, I can see the wheels turning in your head. Smoke is pouring out of your ears. What's all this thought for?"

I looked at him and smiled, "I don't know, a really weird dream last night. Hopefully that won't bode poorly for us tonight?"

"I guess we'll find out." He said, just as Albert walked up to the podium for the night's briefing.

"Ok, settle down!" Albert spouted. Whenever he gave briefings he always seemed to try and puff himself up. It was like an animal trying to make itself look larger I guess. "We have a new memo I have to read tonight. We are now instructed to tell each guest we deal with to see the comedy show."

"What are you talking about?" I asked, "What do you mean I have to tell them about the comedy show?"

"When you end up talking to a guest, management wants you to suggest they go to the Jester's Court and see the show. Tell them it's really good."

"Is it?" I asked.

"Of course it is!" Albert growled back, "But whether or not it is true, you need to tell people it's really good anyway!"

Paul raised his hand beside me, "Shouldn't they be telling Tom this when they escort him down?"

"How about Mr. Funnybuns?" I broke in, "Should we be telling Mr. Funnybuns how good the show is?"

Albert looked confused now, "You need to…..Mr. Funnybuns? What the hell are you two talking about?"

"I ain't dealing with that sum bitch again!" Hank drawled from the back of the room.

"You aren't dealing with who again?" Albert was really confused now.

"Funnybuns my *ass!*" Hank screamed.

"Ok, knock this stuff off!" Albert tried to calm things down, "If you have any problems with what the memo says, take it up with Stan, ok?"

"So what did that memo say?" Matt asked. He had to chime in and make things worse.

"I just told you what it said!" Albert shouted back. "If you have any problems, see Stan! Moving on people, last night we had a heart attack up on the floor. We'll be doing C.P.R. update classes again soon and you people need to pay attention! Last night Robert saved some guy's life because he paid attention!"

Now the whole room looked at me. I didn't care much for the attention. Officers started leaning toward me and asking questions. I just sat there quietly and shortly Albert began screaming for quiet again. "I *said* you people need to pay attention, and I meant at briefing, too!"

"It's busy up on the casino floor. We need to get through this briefing and get

to work!" Albert yelled, "I'm going to skip all these missing people on these
papers so we can skip the stupid questions. If you want to see them, they'll be up

here on the podium."

"Then are they really missing?" Paul asked.

"Can I ask some stupid questions anyway?" Matt asked.

I turned to Paul, "Is this Indiana?" I thought for a few seconds and then asked,

"Do I have a blue ID?" Paul shook his head.

"I give up." Albert said and walked away from the podium.

"He gave up, we win!" I screamed. A small cheer erupted in the briefing

room. Everyone got up slowly and made their way up to the casino, hotel and the

other posts.

Albert hadn't been kidding. When I got on the casino floor it was wall to wall

people. I walked towards the casino cage to check if there were any table game

fills waiting to go out. When a table ran a low on casino chips, a pit clerk would

notify the cage. The chips needed would be set out for Security to take to the

assigned table. This was easy enough if you just made certain the right amount of

chips had been set out. Everybody makes mistakes. The fills came with a slip

that had to be signed by the cage person making the fill, the Security Officer, the

dealer and the floorman, but you as the security officer still had to check and make sure a mistake hadn't been made with the amount. I looked in the fill window and saw it was empty.

The Security Podium, referred to as the "Booth", was right next to the cage. I stopped by to chat with the booth officer. He was talking quietly to Jack.

"Hiya Jack!" I yelled loudly, "Where's the beef?" Jack scowled at me and walked away. I thought back about how I had said I would be good tonight. Oh well.

Tonight's Booth Officer was Jerry. I smirked at him and asked what he had been talking about with Jack.

"He obviously doesn't think you're Prince Charming." Jerry answered.

"Well then," I smiled, "He's severely misinformed, because I *am* Prince Charming!"

Jerry looked at me for a minute and said, "Did you really hit him in the face with liver?"

"Does everybody know about this now?" I asked.

"A big, resounding yes." Jerry said.

I nodded, "He was in the damned way! After the heart attack, C.P.R. and then I get an employee accident, it just wasn't a good night!"

"Yeah, you really did get run around a lot last night. Did you do both the employee accident and the heart attack reports?" Jerry asked.

I shook my head, "Phil did the heart attack for me and I sent the accident to the emergency room with the paramedics. He was supposed to come back for the paperwork when he returned from the hospital. He must have come back after we left so I don't know who did that one." I tried to think about the accident and who might have been assigned the report. All that stood out in my mind was hitting Jack with the liver.

I shrugged at Jerry and walked away to patrol through the crowd. I walked towards the Cloud Nine Lounge with the eerie feeling I was going to see Frank Sinatra and a bunch of cows. Things were normal though, with a band playing up on the small stage. I stopped for a minute to watch and got a quick wave from the female lead singer. I waved back and walked into the lounge to listen to the music for a minute.

I walked through and came across a man leaning across the bar screaming at the bartender. The music was so loud I couldn't hear what he was screaming about. I leaned over to the bartender to ask what was going on, but couldn't hear him either. I tapped the screamer on the shoulder and pointed to the lounge exit. He turned to face me and then began to scream at me. I still couldn't hear what he was saying over all the noise in the lounge. I pointed again, but the man just kept screaming at me. Finally, I grabbed him by the arm and helped him to the lounge exit.

"Now what the hell is all the screaming about?" I shouted.

The man looked at me with wide eyes for a second and then bent over at the waist as if he was bowing to me, then vomited on the floor in front of me as I jumped back. He started to fall over so I grabbed him by the shoulders and steered him towards a trashcan. He puked in the can a bit more, looked up at me, and said something like, "Heeb conna goob and drinkin the slom!" He turned back to the can and puked some more. I don't think I had ever seen anyone vomit this much in my whole life.

I radioed dispatch to let them know what was going on. I wanted them to know I would be tied up dealing with this guy for a little bit. Matt, always one to listen to his radio, came walking over to where we were and asked me what was happening.

"We's slooging the slommy bartender pukie, aren't we?" I smiled as I gave the man a pat on the back. He responded by finding some more puke that went half in and half out of the trashcan. I leaned down and asked the guy if he had any ID on him. He reached into his back pocket and then handed me a wallet. I opened it up and found not only some ID, but also a room key. Luckily it wasn't a Golden Paradise room key. It was for a different hotel, the Stratosphere. That would make things a bit easier. The wallet contained some cash. All we had to do was get the man out to a cab and wave goodbye! Easier said than done. Most cab drivers would refuse to take a puker.

Instead of trying to put the man in a wheelchair and tip off the cabbies that he was drunk, we tried to walk him out the entrance. Things were going well until we got outside. There was a fairly long line for cabs. Damn. We walked the man over and got in line with him. No sense in making other guests mad by cutting the line. As we slowly moved up I noticed the man had puke on the front of his shirt. Nothing like advertising. We got to the front of the line and the first two cabs drove right by the cabstand. The third stopped, got out and began motioning for the next person in line. I stopped the person and told the cabbie to take the drunk. He refused and began to scream at me. I started to walk in front of the cab over to the cabbie, but before I could get to him he jumped back in the cab and drove away still screaming out the window.

Thankfully, the next cab stopped and the driver got out helping us with the drunken man. "He has money?" the cabbie asked me.

"Yup," I answered, "Plenty in his wallet. Just take him to Stratosphere and have their security guys make him pay you." The driver got back into the cab and drove off with the man. One tragedy down, who knew how many more to go. Matt and I walked back inside the crowded casino.

Things were pretty busy and now I heard the familiar call from the Booth officer of "chip fills in the window." I headed that way thinking doing some fills would be a peaceful change from the normal chaos.

I got near the door to the cage and had Jerry buzz the door open. I walked inside. There was only one fill in the window. I called dispatch letting them know I would be out on the fill. I counted it and placed the racks of chips into a small, see-thru box called a "birdcage". I headed out into the casino towards the

pit where it was to be delivered. I was stopped by a visibly unhappy man sitting

in front of a slot machine. He was staring at a small plastic bag filled with
change.

"Hey! Where do I put the coins in this thing?" he asked as I was walking by.

"All our machines are now *coinless*, Sir." I replied, "They only take bills."

"Well change this one back," he said, "I want to play my coins."

I looked at him struggling not to spout any profanity, "It can't be changed

back, Sir, you'll just have to take your coins to the cage and change them into

bills to play."

He glared angrily at me and shouted, "I'm a customer here and I told you to

change it back! Now get your ass to work!"

The night was shaping up to be quite lovely. "I don't have time for this." I

said and walked off toward the pit with my fill. I could hear the man screaming

as I walked away. I ignored him.

I entered the pit and handed the paperwork to the floorman who logged it

down on a sheet in the middle of the pit. I could see the booth from where I was

standing and could still hear the man screaming. He was now screaming at Jerry

in the booth and pointing at the pit where I was standing. I could then hear Jerry

call over the radio for a supervisor to come to the booth for a guest complaint.

Albert responded and said he'd be right there. I turned back to my fill and finished it up, and headed back to the cage with the empty birdcage.

I walked by the booth and back into the main cage. Jerry buzzed the door open for me, and the man pointed at me and started screaming, "That's him, that's him!". I dropped off the birdcage and walked back out into the casino. I ignored the man at the booth as I walked away. He was now screaming, "You're gonna lose your job now, asshole! I'm a customer, so you have to do what I say! Your job's history!"

Another satisfied customer, I thought. I headed towards the 8 Star Club to take my mind off the screaming idiot and saw there was a huge line out front. It was long enough to extend partially into the high limit casino. One of the club bouncers was walking around the line trying to get it a bit more organized. I walked up to the bouncer standing at the entrance and asked him how things were going. A huge Samoan guy named Sammy shook my hand and said, "Pretty good, Bro. Very crowded inside! No problems yet, though. People have been behaving."

"Give it time." I said, "The night's young and so far it hasn't been the best out here in the casino. What's worse is I've only been working for an hour tonight!"

"Lead Three to Wacaster." Albert came across the radio. Lovely, he didn't even know my badge number.

"Go ahead." I answered.

"Come over to the booth a minute, I need to see you."

Oh goodie, I thought. I'll bet I get to listen to the stupid guy scream at me again! I headed back over towards the booth to meet up with Albert and see how much worse he could make the situation.

I arrived at the booth to find Albert holding out a voluntary statement. "I need you to fill this out with your side of the situation."

"What situation?" I asked.

"Why you stopped that guy from playing the machine." He answered.

"What machine?" I asked, "Why I stopped.....what are you even talking about?"

Albert glared at me, "You stopped a guy from playing a slot machine and you need to write down why!"

"Ok, let's take this slow." I started, "Some guy tried to puke on my shoes a bit ago, I put him in a cab and then I did a fill. Which part of that stopped a guy from playing a slot machine?"

Albert looked up at Jerry, "Are you sure it was him?"

Jerry nodded, "He talked to the guy while walking by with a fill, I think."

"And you told him he couldn't play the machine, right?" Albert accused.

"Oh for crying out loud!" I yelled and snatched the voluntary away from Albert. I quickly wrote, *While doing a fill a guest demanded I reconfigure a coinless slot to take coins. I told him that it couldn't be done and continued with my fill.* I handed it back to Albert and glared at him.

"You need to write more than this." Albert said.

I snorted, "No I don't!"

"This is a guest complaint!" Albert growled, "You have to write what happened, not just one sentence!"

"See the word at the top?" I pointed at the voluntary statement, "It says *voluntary*! You understand what that means, right? That means that if I only want to volunteer one sentence, then that's all you get! And I don't even have to provide that if I don't want to!"

"I'm a *supervisor*!" Albert shouted, "You can't say that to me!"

I began to chuckle to myself, held up a hand, and waved. "Bye, Albert." I said and walked back into the casino. Albert was about to come after me, I think, when we heard Jack calling for dispatch to roll the paramedics.

"111 to Control, roll the paramedics to the Cloud Nine Lounge! Unconscious female with possible alcohol poisoning!"

"Copy 111. Control to all units we will be going into 33 traffic for a medical emergency at the Cloud Nine Lounge. 220, head out the main entrance to bring in paramedics."

33 traffic meant that if you weren't involved in the medical emergency and you didn't have another emergency yourself, you were supposed to stay off the radio. I acknowledged dispatch sending me out to bring in the paramedics and headed for the main entrance.

Alcohol poisoning, I thought to myself. I wondered once again if Jack was blowing something else out of proportion. The main entrance was busy, but things were moving along and I didn't have to move any cars out of the way for the paramedics to park. Maybe things were looking up tonight for a change. While waiting patiently Matt came out to help bring in the fire department. On medical calls both an ambulance and fire department rescue truck would be sent.

"Hi, Matt!" I said, "How's your night going? I've already got my first guest complaint!"

"Do tell!" he said, "Was that what Albert wanted you at the booth for?"

I nodded, "Some guy said I stopped him from playing a slot machine."

"You Monster!" Matt smiled.

"Did you pass by the lounge and see at all what was going on there with Jack?" I asked.

"No," Matt answered, "I just came out here. I'm sure we'll get to see what's going on when we take in the medics."

"111 to units outside, I need the paramedics in here a.s.a.p.! Her boyfriend says if they don't show up right away, his father will be really pissed!"

I couldn't resist this, "Who's his father?" I asked over the radio. No response. I couldn't wait to get back inside with the paramedics now and see Jack in person. I could hear sirens now and watched as an ambulance drove past the casino and up the Strip. Paul was following them on his bike.

"Bike 3 to Control, the ambulance just drove on by. I don't think they know where they're going!" Paul called over the radio.

"Maybe they weren't for us?" I called back.
The ambulance now turned around and drove back the other way. Paul followed along on his bike. Finally, Paul stopped following the ambulance. He got off his bike at the drive coming up to the main entrance. The ambulance drove by again. As it went by Paul began waving his arms and shined his flashlight at the ambulance. The ambulance continued up the street and headed for one of the hotel's side entrances. Paul looked up at Matt and I and shrugged his shoulders as we began laughing. He put his hands on his hips and waited to see if the ambulance would come back.

"Hurry up the ambulance!" Jack screamed over the radio, "She's coming around and her boyfriend said his father is going to be really mad at how long this is taking!"

"Who's his father?" I asked again over the radio.

"His father is…..what Sir? Yes, they're on their way right now!" Jack answered.

The ambulance came driving back up from the side of the hotel and turned in the drive where Paul was standing. "Are you guys idiots?" Paul yelled as he followed them up to the main entrance.

The ambulance pulled up and the paramedics got out. "What's the status?"

one asked me.

"Maybe the patient is dead now because you can't pay attention to where you're being directed to pull in?" Paul said as he rode up on his bike. The paramedic glared at him.

"I don't really know." I answered the paramedic, trying to hide a smile. I was just sent to bring you guys inside."

The two paramedics unloaded a gurney from the back of the ambulance and I led them into the casino. Matt went up to meet the fire department as we headed inside. We arrived at the lounge to find a female sitting up on a chair looking a bit pale. "So," one paramedic asked, "What's going on?"

"Can't you see she's sick? A guy nearby started screaming, "You people need to fix her!"

"What's the problem?" the paramedic asked the male again.

"She's sick, I said! Can't you hear? Don't you know who my father is?" the man continued screaming.

"Who *is* your father?" I asked.

The man ignored me and pulled out a cell phone, "I'm calling my host! Nobody treats us like this, I'm telling my father!"

The paramedics asked the girl how much she had to drink tonight. She said she didn't know. She seemed really drunk to me, though. The guy kept screaming into the cell phone. Finally, the paramedics asked the girl if she wanted to go to the hospital. She shook her head. "Well then there's not much we can do for you." The paramedics began to pack their stuff up and headed towards the main entrance. They met the fire department coming in and told them what was going on. The fire department turned around and walked back out the main entrance also.

"Hey!" the guy screamed at them, "She's still sick! You have to do something! You don't just walk away like this! I pay taxes! Do you know who my father is?"

Matt had walked up now, "Who is his father?" he asked me.

"His father is the man in charge of the sock department at Sears in Muncie, Indiana!" I announced and walked off laughing. I could still hear the man screaming at Jack and maybe I should have stayed to help out. Part of me didn't want to stay. Another part of me was certain I'd start laughing and get another guest complaint when this guy started screaming about his father to me. Better to move along. I headed towards the 8 Star to see if anything interesting was going on there.

On my way towards the club the familiar call for fills came from Jerry at the booth. I changed course and headed to the cage. Jerry buzzed the door open and I went in to find five fills sitting there this time waiting to be done. Nobody seemed to want to do them. I wondered where the other casino units were as I checked the fills and loaded them into a cart.

I walked out towards a pit to do the first fill and heard dispatch come over the radio: "Fight at the 8 Star! We've got a major fight out front, Control to 220!" I'd already told dispatch I was doing the fills, why were they calling me now?

"220 to Control, I'll get to the fight after the fills I'm doing." I said calmly.

"Control copies, any available floor units respond to the 8 Star!"

Matt responded and said he was headed over. No response from any other unit. I thought to myself how one day these other guys might need back up. How could you expect someone that you wouldn't back up to help you if you were in trouble? I continued with my fills and just shook my head.

"501 to Control, I'm at the club. There are two guys fighting here." Cortez came over the radio.

"Copy 501, you want to break them up?" Control asked.

"501 to Control, they're hitting each other in the face!" Cortez mumbled.

"187 making contact!" Matt screamed over the radio. I could imagine him jumping in between the two people fighting as Cortez watched.

I entered the pit and waited for the floorman to come over and log the fill on a pit sheet. Finally, the pit boss walked over and looked at me, "Something seems to be going on over at the club. Can you tell what's going on?" he asked me.

"I don't know," I said, "I'm just doing fills."

More commotion on the radio. Two or three officers were trying to talk at the same time so you couldn't hear anything but static. Finally Matt came across

sounding really upset, "Do *something*, you idiot! Take him into custody!" I

wanted to finish the fills quickly and run over to help, but there were 4 left to do.
Once I had signed for them, I had to finish them.

"Two going to the C.S.O." Matt finally said sounding a bit calmer.

Finishing the fills took me another 20 minutes. I headed towards the 8 Star to

see if I could find out what had happened. I arrived to find Sammy with a large

wet spot across the front of his shirt, "What the hell happened?" I asked.

"Stupid punk got rowdy inside. When they were walking him out here, he

threw his drink at me!" he answered.

"Threw his drink at you?" I repeated, "Did he hit you with the glass at all?"

"Oh yeah, but I'm fine, no damage. I just got a little wet." The Samoan said,
smiling.

"Did they give you a voluntary to fill out about what happened?" I asked him.

"It all happened inside." Sammy replied.

"He hit you with his drink!" I said, "You need to fill out *something* for us!

That's at least assault and battery! That at least justifies us to 86 him!"

He looked at me for a minute and then agreed. I said I would bring him a

clipboard and let him fill it out while still watching the club door. I headed over

to the C.S.O. for a voluntary and to let Matt know. I neared the door and saw

Cortez standing outside. I glanced at him and then entered the C.S.O. Cortez peeked inside behind me as I walked in. Matt started screaming at him: "You get

the hell out of here, you *son of a bitch*!"

I looked at Matt and then at the two men in handcuffs sitting on the C.S.O.
bench. You could tell they had both been in a fight and were going to look a lot

worse in the morning. One guy had a trickle of blood coming from the corner of

his mouth. The other had a slight cut on his forehead that was bleeding. They

were both going to swell up quite nicely.

"What the hell was that all about?" I asked Matt.

"When I got to the fight Cortez just stood there! And when I broke em' up, he

still just stood there and didn't help at all!" Matt screamed.

"Hey," the guy with the cut forehead started to speak up, "I didn't do....."

Matt turned on him right away, "You shut the hell up! Everything in here is

recorded, but I still don't want to hear a fucking word out of you until the

supervisor gets here!"

"Called Stan?" I asked.

"Yeah," Matt answered, "He's on his way."

I picked up a voluntary and told Matt about the club bouncer being hit with the

drink. He nodded and I walked back out of the C.S.O. with a clipboard and the

voluntary. I passed Stan as I was coming out.

"What's going on?" he asked me.

"See Matt." I answered, "I was on fills, and this is his show. Be warned, he's all pissed off." Stan nodded and headed on in.

I heard the call of more fills come over the radio so I dropped off the voluntary to the bouncer and headed towards the cage. I called Matt and told him he would have to pick up the voluntary from the bouncer while I did fills.

I walked by the Security Booth and saw Albert standing there. He looked up at me and it looked as though he was about to say something to me. I ignored him and walked into the cage for the fills. I loaded up a couple fills and wheeled the cart out of the cage and into a furious looking Albert blocking my way to the pits.

"You need to fill out another voluntary!" he said to me with his hands on his hips.

"Why?" I asked, "What happened to the other one I filled out?"

"I threw it away!" He yelled, "You need to write more than you did!"

I just looked at him for a minute and then said, "No." I walked around him and headed for the pits. I could hear him yelling behind me as I walked away, ignoring him. *Another night in Paradise* I mused to myself.

"Lead Three to Wacaster," he blustered over the radio, "After you're done with those fills report to the Booth and do another voluntary!"

I shook my head. He apparently wasn't going to leave me alone. I ignored the call and tried to think of something to write which would just make him madder. I finished the fills. I dropped the fill cart off in the cage and walked back out to the Booth. Albert was nowhere to be seen so I went over to talk to Jerry.

"Give me another voluntary." I said holding out my hand.

"How many pages would you like?" Jerry asked, "Or will this just be the same short thing you wrote last time?"

"Short, but not the same." I replied. I took the voluntary he held out and wrote, *"This voluntary statement is to reiterate that the last voluntary statement I filled out is true to my recollection of the situation."* I handed it back to Jerry and told him to make sure Albert got it.

"You know this is just going to piss him off." Jerry said reading what I had written.

"Well then," I smiled back, "I'll warm up my violin!"

"Control to 220, are you clear?"

I always hated it when someone asked me that. It always meant they were going to send me on something I probably didn't want to do and no one else could do.

"Affirmative Control, what do you want now?"

"Pick up some paperwork and head over to Ambrosia for a guest complaint."

"Ambrosia?" I asked, "Shouldn't an R and S unit be taking that?"

"They requested you. They remember you from last night, I guess. The head Chef called and requested *Robert*."

"Lovely." I replied, "On my way. Any idea what the complaint is?"

"Unknown at this time." Came the reply though I swear I could hear a snicker in the background.

I arrived at the Ambrosia to find an officer named Fred standing at a table speaking with 4 guys. I saw the Chef over by the kitchen motioning me over. I headed for him first.

He started screaming about the table of guys as I neared him, "Zay eat food off ze plate of *three different* orders! Each time zay say it is no good and now zay say zay will not pay! Robair, I want you to hit zem vis ze liver like when she escape yesterday!"

I stood looking at him with my mouth open for at least 30 seconds.

"Henry….uh….Chef….I got in trouble for that yesterday, I'm not supposed to hit anybody with meat anymore."

"*Zay say zay will not pay!*" He yelled back at me, "Zay are dogs vis no taste! I vill use ze escaped liver zen!" he screamed and stormed back into the kitchen.

"Henry?" I called after him, "Chef Henry, calm down a minute. Come back here!"

He came back out of the kitchen with a large handful of raw liver. He cocked back his arm in an effort to throw the liver across the restaurant at the table of guys.

"Henry, NO!" I screamed, "What the hell is the matter with you?" I grabbed his arm. He fought to get loose and throw the liver.

"Henry, stop this nonsense! At least let me try to work it out!" I pleaded.

"Hey Cook!" one of the guys yelled, "What's that you've got there; is that some more dog you're going to burn?" The whole group started laughing hysterically. Somehow Henry's arm got loose and he threw the liver. It missed the table and he then started yelling French at them. Henry tried harder to get past me and get to the table.

"How about frying up some cat to go with that dog you just tossed?" one guy yelled. The table continued to laugh. I glanced over while still trying to get control of Henry and noticed Fred was laughing along with them.

"God Damn it, Fred!" I screamed, "You want to shut those idiots up and get them out of here?"

Henry continued the fight to get away from me and kept screaming something in French I could only assume was all the French swear words and curses he knew.

I managed to get one hand up to my radio button and pleaded for some competent backup.

"Control to 220, backup's on the way. What's the situation there?" I squeezed the button and let Henry's French curses go out over the air for about 15 seconds. I let go and went back to using both hands to try and wrestle Henry back into the kitchen. Fred was still just standing near the table of hecklers not doing anything. *Only one thing could make this worse*, I thought to myself. Be careful what you wish for….And then Jack and Cortez showed up for back up.

"Hey, what's going on here?" Cortez asked as he sauntered up to the table near Fred. Jack followed him over to the table of laughing drunks, neither officer coming over to help me with the screaming, struggling chef.

"Are you throwing some more meat around?" Jack asked looking towards me, "Is that meat on the floor trying to escape?"

I almost let go of Henry and helped him attack the table. Part of me kept focus on my job though, and I muscled Henry back into the kitchen. I could hear Jack, Cortez and Fred still near the table laughing with the drunks.

"*Stop this bullshit now!*" I screamed at Henry, "You're a fucking world renowned chef, not some common street thug! Do you really want me to let you out there to attack four drunken idiots with no taste because they were teasing you?"

Henry stopped fighting and looked up at me. "What vas I supposed to do? Yesterday you are ze one who throw ze meat!"

Now I felt like an ass. I took a deep breath and thought about what to say, "Look Henry….I'm just a dumb security officer and that wasn't even acceptable from me. I got in trouble for it and it shouldn't have happened. You called for me to come take care of this; and then didn't even bother to let me even try! If someone needs to be hit with liver, at least let me, the dumb security guy do it!"

"Lead Three to units at the Ambrosia, what's going on over there?" I could hear Albert finally calling over the radio. Someone from management was now going to mishandle the situation, goodie.

"As far as I can tell at the moment Sir, four guests are refusing to pay their bill and harassing the Chef." I said into the radio.

"I'm on my way, stand by." Albert responded.

Jack appeared in the kitchen doorway, "Hey, were you really cooking dog in here?"

"Cooking *dog?*" he screamed and started moving towards a rack of knives hanging in the kitchen. I stepped between him and the knives.

"Henry, calm *down!*" I said again, "Jack, get the hell out of here and get some I.D. from those drunks at the table!"

"Oui Li-vair Boy!" Henry screamed at Jack, "You are not welcome in my kitchen! You leave at once before I bake you into a pie!"

Jack looked angry, but left the kitchen and went back out to the table. Albert had arrived and was now talking to the four drunks with Fred and Cortez.

"Listen Henry," I said, "I'll go out and make sure these guys pay and then leave, ok? I'll handle the security guys and whatever needs to be done with this, but I need you to stay in here, ok?"

Henry looked me in the face and asked, "Do you think I cook dog in here?"

"Oh please," I answered, "I've read the reviews of this restaurant and how you cook. The things you guys create in here are considered to be works of art to people with taste! Don't let four drunks who probably think grade C meat is good eatin'! They aren't well to do people, they aren't food critics, they're just drunks. Worry about the people that matter, ok?"

Henry looked at me for a while and then finally said, "You are right, Robair. Zey have no taste and only want cheap wine! To hell vis zem! You make me feel good, I like you!"

"I like you too, Henry." I said, "Now can you stay in here while I handle this, please?" He nodded as I walked back out into the restaurant. I had lied to Henry about reading reviews of his cooking and the restaurant, but what the hell. It had calmed him down and helped resolve things peacefully....for now.

On my way to the table I picked up the liver that was still lying on the floor. I held on to it as I walked over towards the table. Albert had been talking to the four guys, but everyone stopped as I walked up.

"I'm told you guys ordered 3 meals and now don't want to pay for them." I said.

"It's ok, it's gonna be code 4 this time." Albert said.

"So they paid?" I asked.

"No, but they said the food was a bit undercooked, so we'll let it go this time."

I looked at Albert. "Three meals were undercooked by the Ambrosia's Chef?"

"I *said* its code 4!" Albert insisted.

"Ok, you're the supervisor." I scowled, "The Chef is pretty upset, though.

Would you like to speak with *him* about this matter?"

I looked over at Jack, Cortez and Fred. They were all standing together. I reared back my arm as if to throw the liver at them and screamed, "Raaaahhh!" All three took a couple steps backward. I noticed as I walked out of The Ambrosia everyone in the restaurant was staring at me. Every person in the place had probably been watching me since I had started trying to push Henry back into the kitchen.

"See you around, *Liver Boy!*" I said to no one in particular as I tossed the raw liver in a trash can on my way out of the restaurant.

Maybe there were some more fills in the window I could do for a little bit of solitude, I thought. I headed back towards the cage trying not to think about the Ambrosia. I took my time and watched the people around me. Maybe some quiet for a bit? Not a chance:

"Control to 220." Phooey.

"220, go ahead, what is it this time?"

"Landline Ambrosia or go back over there. Chef Henry wants to speak to you."

What the hell did Henry want now? I wanted to stay in the casino and do nice, quiet fills! Being busy meant the night went by quickly, but sometimes it just stressed me out. I found a house phone and called The Ambrosia.

"Ambrosia fine dining featuring Chef *Honray Lepardue*, how may I help you?" a pleasant female voice answered. She pronounced Henry's name correctly. I always mispronounced it by calling him Henry but he still insisted on

having me deal with all his problems. Sheesh.

"Hi, this is Robert from security, I was told the Chef wanted to speak to me." I heard elevator music coming through the phone as she put me on hold to transfer

me to the kitchen.

"Oui?" someone answered in French.

"This is Robert in Security, Chef Henry asked for me to call him." I tried. I

wondered how much English the other French guys in the back actually spoke.

He spouted off some French I didn't understand and I heard him set down the

phone. A minute later Henry answered.

"Robair?" He shouted, "Ze Livair Boy and some fat Italian pig vill not leave

my kitchen! I want you to get zem out *now*!" he hung up the phone.

A fat Italian pig. It had to be Albert. Chef Henry was supposed to be dealt

with carefully and we were to help him with anything he asked. I knew Albert

wouldn't listen to me if I went over there and told him to leave. It was time to use

my head. I picked up the phone and dialed.

"Security, Stan Truman speaking." A jolly voice answered.

"Hi Stan, it's Robert." I said nicely.

"Robert!" he said happily, "You've been pretty busy tonight, I've been

listening to the radio!"

"Uh, yeah. I need some supervisory help now." I almost pleaded.

"I see," Stan said still sounding really happy, "And what can I do for you? Do you need some discipline or something? An extra day off? Help getting Matthew off some girl?"

"Well I…." I began, "Did you say help getting Matthew off a girl?"

Stan just laughed, "What do you need, Robert?"

"Has anybody told you about what was going on in the Ambrosia?" I asked.

"Albert was supposed to be handling that. I just know what I heard on the radio. Please try not to let the Chef scream French over the air again, ok?"

I smiled at that, "Well 4 guys at a table ordered something and sent it back, I guess. I was told they did this with three different orders and then refused to pay for any of it. The Chef got all upset and it got a bit out of control. I didn't get to talk to the four guys because after I got Henry all calmed down, Albert arrived and told me it was code 4 and to leave. So I did. Now the Chef is screaming for me to get Jack and some *Fat Italian pig* out of his kitchen. I don't have any authority over a supervisor, so….."

"So you'd like me to get the Fat Italian pig out of the kitchen for you, right? Stan finished for me with a little chuckle.

"Yeah, that's it." I answered, "By the way, how did the fight Matthew broke up end?"

"Nobody wanted to press charges, no witnesses, non-hotel guests, so I just trespassed them and let them leave. Matt wasn't very happy about that, but we have other things to worry about."

"You can say that again." I said, "I can't wait for my lunch just so I can sit down for a minute!"

"And eat some *bad tuna*?" Stan chuckled, "I'll take care of Albert for you, go and sit down somewhere for a few minutes."

"Thanks." I said with a sigh, "I really appreciate it. I hung up and a minute later heard Stan calling Albert on the radio asking him for a landline.

I walked back into the casino and took a slow walk by the lounge. Typically, there were a few working girls hanging around. One I actually recognized. I usually didn't pay much attention to the hookers, but every once in a while there were one or two who would give me a lot of trouble if I asked for ID. I would always remember them. This one was named "Theresa" and was only 19 years old.

"Hey!" I interrupted her as she was talking to a prospective client, "How many times have you been 86'ed from this place?" The guy she was talking to looked up at me surprised.

"I don't know what you're talking about," she lied, "I've never been 86'ed from anyplace!"

"Let's see some ID, and when it says you're 19 years old I'm going to take you to the C.S.O. I will call vice so they can arrest you for being near a bar, a gaming area, and whatever else they think you're doing *illegally*!" I spouted.

"I…..ah…..I left it in my car." She stammered.

"Ok, no more games, Theresa." I tried to puff myself all up for the same old game, "Hit the door, you know you can't be in here." I looked over at the guy she was with, "By the way, I'm told she has about 3 different S.T.D.'s. Some of them here have H.I.V., so maybe you should consider going to a legal place outside Clark County. Much cleaner and safer."

"I don't have any of those whatever you just said!" Theresa yelled at me.

"Didn't I just tell you to hit the door?" I asked pulling out my handcuffs.

Theresa stuck her tongue out at me and started walking towards the main entrance. I followed along to make sure she got outside.

"This is just business you know," she snarled at me, "You don't have to get personal about things!"

I chuckled to myself but didn't say anything and continued to follow her to the door. She opened a cell phone and began to call someone, probably her pimp. I followed her out the door and to the cab line. She stayed on the phone until she got into a cab and rode away. I went back into the casino.

I strolled through the main casino and then headed towards the high limit casino by the main tower. I walked a slow circle around the high limit casino and then walked absent-mindedly towards the lounge again. There Theresa was, back at the lounge chatting with another guy!

I walked up to her again, "I just watched you get into a cab! What the hell are you doing back in here?" I screamed

"I'm part of the entertainment." She said calmly, "You guys should give me a nametag."

"What the hell is wrong with you?" I screamed again, "Get the hell out of here and stay out this time!"

"You know, you're just mean!" she said as she got up again.

This time I pulled the trespass card out of my pocket that we were required to read to people being 86'ed, "As a duly appointed representative....."

"Yeah, yeah." She said as she walked towards the door, "Why do you always have to read that? It's getting a bit boring now!"

I finished reading the card. I called dispatch to let them know I was walking her out a second time. They acknowledged me and once again I watched her get into a cab. This time I stood by and made sure the cab drove away. At least I thought it was driving away. It stopped at the corner. She got out and started walking back towards the casino! This girl really had guts!! I put my hands on my hips and stood near the cab line watching and waiting until she got back near the entrance.

I sighed and crossed my arms as she came near. She looked over in my direction with a mock look of shock on her face.

Without a word she turned and walked back towards the corner. I continued to watch her go. When she finally got to the corner she turned, looked at me again, and stuck out her tongue. I still stood there watching until she crossed the street and entered another casino. I hoped that would be the last I'd see of her tonight

"Control to 220, if you're all done chasing the working girls, you're clear for break."

Apparently dispatch had been watching me on camera the entire time, enjoying the show.

Lovely, I thought. Lunchtime had finally come. Maybe I could get a little bit of peace while I got something to munch. Matt had been cleared for lunch also. I met up with him as I headed for the employee dining area. We decided to make a quick stop at a restroom before eating. We walked in and heard shouting. It sounded like a scuffle. We found two Mexican employees having a fistfight! I grabbed one and Matt grabbed the other. We pulled them apart.

"What the hell is going on here?" I screamed. The two men screamed Spanish at each other and continued to try to get at each other. This just wasn't going to be my night.

"Lock em' down!" I screamed at Matt as I shoved the man I had a hold of towards the wall. "Hands behind your back!" I screamed at him as I pulled out my handcuffs.

"220 to Lead One." I said over the radio.

"Lead One, go ahead." Stan answered.

"Two employees in restraints for fighting in the men's room. Can you meet us in the C.S.O.?" I said as we began walking the two men back upstairs.

"Ok, I'll be there." Stan answered

"What the hell is this shit all about?" I asked the man I was leading along.

"No English." He replied.

"No English, huh?" I scowled, "I wonder how you applied for and got a job here."

We took the two men upstairs and walked them past a few staring hotel guests to the C.S.O.. I used my key to open the door and told the dispatchers to make the room "hot."

"Sit down!" I pointed to a bench with a padded wall behind it.

The man I had placed in cuffs looked at me and said, "I didn't do nothing!"

"Suddenly you speak English, huh?" I answered, "You must be a quick study."

The man Matt had brought in said something to the other man in Spanish and they began to argue again.

"Both of you shut the hell up!" I screamed, "I want absolute silence until I ether get your supervisors in here, or a translator! Now, quiet!"

I sat down at the C.S.O. desk, picked up the phone, and called dispatch. Joey answered, "How's your lunch going so far?" he giggled.

"You're going to be alone with me out there tomorrow," I growled, "So watch the smart remarks."

"No, I won't," he replied happily, "I traded with Matt! You'll be out here alone with *him* tomorrow!" I looked over at Matt.

Matt looked back over at me, "What?" he asked.
"You traded with Joey for tomorrow?" I asked.

"Of course!" he replied, "We always work well out there together! We always have fun, don't we?"

"Yeah, I guess so." I pouted. "Ok, send me a Spanish translator because these guys supposedly don't speak any English." I said into the phone to Joey.

"You got it." He said and hung up the phone. I heard him call Cortez to respond to the C.S.O.. *Lovely*, I thought.

A couple of minutes later Stan came in the C.S.O. followed by Cortez. "Ok, talk to me." Stan said as he sat down at the desk next to me.

"We entered the bathroom downstairs trying to wash up for lunch and these two guys were throwing punches." I answered.

"*We* being you and Matt, correct?" Stan asked. We both nodded. "Have you called their supervisor yet?" he asked.

"No," I replied, "They say they don't speak any English, so we were waiting for a translator."

"I see." Stan said and looked at the two men in cuffs. "So what do you two have to say?"

Before they could answer, the phone rang. Stan picked it up and after a minute looked at me, "It's for you, *Robair*!"

I stood there for a minute, almost afraid to take the phone. "Hello?" I finally said.

"Robair!" Came Henry's familiar voice, "Ze fat Italian pig is now itting on ze waitresses! You vill come and get him away from here now!"

"Henry….." I tried.

"No!" He spouted back, "You tell me you are ze security to throw ze livair, not me! You vill come and get ze pig off ze waitress NOW!" He hung up.

I stood there holding the phone while Stan, Matt, and the two men in cuffs watched me. I fought the urge to throw the receiver across the room. Instead, I gently hung up the phone and turned to Stan, "Chef Henry says Albert is bothering the waitresses at the Ambrosia and he wants me to make him leave."

"If he is bothering the waitresses, shouldn't they be the ones complaining?" Matt asked.

I glared at him and noticed a small smile cross his lips.

"Lead One to Lead Three." Stan said over his radio.

"Lead Three, go ahead." Albert answered.

"Come to the C.S.O. and give me a hand with these fighting employees, please." Stan said as he winked at me. "This should tie him up for a little while."

"Yeah, I guess." I answered, "At least I've been leaving Jack alone tonight."

"And don't think I don't appreciate that!" Stan laughed.

A few minutes later Albert walked into the C.S.O.. He glanced in my direction and said, "Hey, I've been looking for you! That voluntary wasn't funny! I told you to fill out another one, and I meant it!"

"I filled two out already!" I yelled back, "Use the first one I gave you!"

"I threw that one away!" he yelled back, "It wasn't good enough!"

"It…..what?" I stammered, "It wasn't good enough? It was supreme! It was the greatest piece of writing ever done! It should have been published, given an ISBN #, placed in libraries, and book stores right next to the Holy Bible!"

"Robert….." Stan said.

"Angels sang when I wrote that!" I continued to yell, "The heavens above opened up and light fell down on the paper, people applauded. I was given a standing ovation for what I wrote!"

"Robert….." Stan said again.

"Shakespeare himself climbed out of his grave and signed off on that voluntary…..!" I continued to scream.

"*Robert!*" Stan screamed, "Can I see you outside for a minute, please?"

I stopped yelling and looked at Stan, "Sure, no need to get all excited." We walked outside the C.S.O.

"You know it's recorded in there and you know not to get all worked up like that. Not only in front of a supervisor, but in the C.S.O., don't you?" Stan asked.

"Yeah, but….." I tried to explain.

"Since you know better I expect you to act like it!" Stan said, "Now what voluntary is he talking about?"

"Some guest complaint." I said, "Some guy was mad because I didn't fix a machine to take his change. I was on fills and didn't stop to talk to the guy for long. I wrote him a short voluntary. He obviously didn't like it and probably threw it away. Now he wants another one."

"Ok, I'll talk to Albert," Stan said, "You fill out another voluntary for him, fill one out for this fight and get them to me after you take your lunch, ok?"

"Another one?" I whined, "But I already….."

"*Get me the voluntaries after your lunch!*" Stan insisted.

"Yes Sir." I answered.

"Now go to lunch and try to relax a bit." he said, "I'll have Matt finish up with the two employees and we'll have Albert do the report. Then I'll send him down to lunch, too. Now go take it easy for a bit! You're getting all stressed out tonight!"

I nodded and walked back towards the employee dining room in the basement. Once in the dining room, I piled a bunch of food onto my plate and sat down at a table. I just stared at it and pouted. I tried taking a bite or two but didn't really feel like eating. After all that has happened to me tonight I was letting a stupid voluntary bother me. Guest complaints were a pain in the butt!

Finally, after eating about half the food I decided to just scribble those voluntaries and get them out of the way. I dumped the other half of my food and got myself a glass of chocolate milk. I took it into the briefing room with me and started to write. First I wrote one to make myself feel better. It said; "*I have no knowledge of anything that has ever, or will ever goes on inside the Golden Paradise Casino and Hotel.*" I signed the voluntary and fought the urge to push it under Stan's door. Finally after deciding to be a good boy and keep my job I wrote; "*While doing fills a guest asked me to alter a coinless slot. I informed him I could not do that and continued on with my fills.*" I wanted to write a few smart ass comments about how this was the third voluntary I had filled out for the same incident. I figured Stan would probably get upset. Since he had cut me a bit of slack after hitting Jack with the liver, I had better behave at least for a little while and just, "keep it professional."

I scribbled out another voluntary about how Matt and I had come across the two guys fighting in the bathroom and then shoved both voluntaries under Stan's closed office door. Once through with the voluntaries I sat down in a chair and tried to relax for the rest of my lunch. I could hear the radio crackling constantly, but since the calls weren't for me it was like background noise.

There was a small TV connected to a VCR in the briefing room that was used to show training videos occasionally. I turned it on and tuned into an episode of Cops. I sat back down and closed my eyes trying again to relax. I could hear some guy on the TV screaming he was innocent and nothing was his fault. A small chuckle escaped me. The phone on the briefing room wall began to ring. I ignored it and kept my eyes closed. It rang about 9 times or so and then stopped. Then the radio crackled once again:

"Control to 220, what's your current location?"

I ignored Control and didn't bother to answer. I knew they would keep calling me, but still didn't want to answer.

"Control to 220?" the call came again.

"220, What do you want Control?" I finally answered.

"What's your location?" he asked again.

They weren't even going to let me have a peaceful lunch! I thought for a minute about where I could be and finally answered, "Somewhere in the Antarctic."

"Well, when you pass a landline give me a call, please." Came the non-phased answer.

I let out a sigh and looked up at the TV. The guy who had been yelling he was innocent was now on the ground in handcuffs crying. Lovely scene, I could imagine it going on right now out in front of the 8 Star Club. I had around 20 minutes of my lunch left and wasn't going to call the dispatchers before my entire lunch hour was up! In fact, since the dispatch office was just down the hallway from the briefing room I decided to walk down there and see what they wanted in person.

I walked out of the briefing room and down the hall. A small cart honked its horn and drove past me carrying a bunch of vegetables. It was heading in the direction I was going and I had to fight the urge to jump on and ride down the hallway.

I arrived at the door that said, "Security Dispatch" and stood staring at it for a minute. Finally, I used my key and walked inside. The room was full of monitors and you could see places throughout the casino and the restaurants. There were even a couple of monitors looking inside the 8 Star Club. The only sounds were the radio playing and Ozzy and Joey talking, though. I glanced up at the monitor looking into the C.S.O. and noticed it was empty. Matt and Stan must have finished with the two guys.

"So what the hell do you guys want this time?" I said with a smile. I sat down in a chair and leaned back.

"What are you so crabby about?" Ozzy asked, "You always say being busy makes the night go by fast."

"Busy, yes," I answered, "Bothered, no. Everything you've given me tonight has just been a big pain in the ass!"

"Well, you can sit and relax for the next detail." Ozzy said, "I want you to relieve the Booth Officer for his lunch after you're clear."

"Right, Booth when I'm clear." I said closing my eyes and leaning back in the chair.

The phones began to ring. Both Ozzy and Joey had to answer lines. Even though both of them were on the phone I could still hear them ringing. I opened my eyes and looked up to see several lines lit up. A part of me almost dreaded my two upcoming nights in here. I closed my eyes again and tried to picture somewhere peaceful. I couldn't come up with anything.

A few minutes later all the calls had been answered, if only for the time being. "So you guys have been pretty busy out here tonight, huh?" I asked with a smile.

"You mean besides all the things we've been sending you on?" Ozzy replied, "Not to mention the things you found on your own?"

"Hey, somebody's got to take care of things here." I replied and stood up, "Would you rather Cortez handle the fights? I put my hands on my hips. He can arrive and announce, *"I'm Cortez Domingo! You will now stop fighting!"* He can run and hide behind a curtain somewhere." Joey began to laugh at this.

"Maybe he should be wearing tights and a cape with a big CD on the chest?" I continued. Joey laughed even harder.

The phones began to ring again. They never seemed to stop in dispatch. I knew I wouldn't get any peace there. I decided to end my lunch and headed to the Security Booth to relieve Jerry.

When I arrived I found Jerry standing there sounding really mad as he spoke to a man standing in front of the booth. "I told you, I don't have it here!" he was saying.

I entered the booth and told Jerry to go to lunch. He turned and walked away in a huff.

"Hi, I'm Robert!" I beamed, "How can I help you?"
"I lost my phone!" the man bellowed at me.

"I see." I answered.

I stood there staring at the man. After about a minute he asked, "Where is it?"

"Where is what?" I asked back.

"Where is my phone!" he screamed back.

"You just told me you lost it." I answered.

"They said they had it and I want it back!" he screamed.

"I want you to have it back," I smiled, "Who are *they*?"

"THEY!" he screamed at me, "The guys that answered my phone!"

"More than one person answered your phone?" I asked in mock shock, "It must be some kind of miracle speakerphone, isn't it? How many *theys* were there?"

"GIVE ME MY PHONE!" the man now screamed at me.

"I don't have your phone. They do, just like you said." I calmly replied.

The man looked furious. I was enjoying myself though, hoping this would continue.

"Why won't you give me my phone back?" he growled again.

"They have it." I replied simply.

"Where's your supervisor?" he demanded.

"I don't know." I answered honestly, "Actually there are three of them, but I'm not sure where any of them are right now."
"I want to see one, NOW!" he screamed at me.

"You know," I looked up into the air thoughtfully, "I think I'd honestly like to see one right now myself."

The man stood there glaring at me. After another minute or two he yelled, "Well, are you going to call him, or not?"

"Call who?" I played dumb.

"Your supervisor!" the man screamed.

"Oh, for a minute there I thought you wanted me to call "*they*" who answered your phone. I don't know who *they* are, so I wouldn't actually be able to call them."

"I'm going to have your job!" the man screamed as he turned and stomped away.

"Yes!" I beamed out as he left, "This place truly is Paradise!" I sat down in the booth chair and looked out around the casino. Same old place, but somehow it always looked differently from the booth. The phone rang and I answered it:

"Security Booth, this is Robert."

"Hi Robert," the caller said politely to me, "I stayed in your hotel about two months ago and I left a shirt in the room."

"You left a shirt in your hotel room two months ago?" I repeated the statement as a question.

"Yes, and I was wondering if it had been turned in to lost and found?" he replied.

"Uh, I'm sorry Sir," I said, "Nothing is kept in lost and found beyond 30 days. Have you called about the shirt earlier?"

"No I haven't called earlier, I just noticed the shirt missing." He replied.

"You stayed here two months ago and just now realized a shirt is missing, so you think it was left here. Am I correct in this?" I asked.

"Hey! I know I left it there!" the man said, "I just didn't know until now! I took that shirt to Vegas and now it's gone!"

"I see," I said, wishing I could reach through the phone and use two fingers to poke the man in the eyes. Just like Moe would do to Curly in a Three Stooges film, "Even so, we don't keep any lost and found longer than 30 days Sir, so if it was found we wouldn't have it any more."

"But I stayed there and anything left in my room should have had my name put on it and saved for me!" he argued.

"Perhaps it wasn't turned in, though." I tried, "Let me check. What's your name and what room number were you staying in?"

"My name is Rupert Trent, and I don't know what room I was in, that was two months ago!"

"All right Mr. Trent," I said nicely, "Let me put you on hold while I check lost and found." I pushed the hold button and set the receiver down. Many people walked up to the booth, asked where the restroom was, so I pointed it out. I watched a cocktail waitress casually walk by. I noticed a few young girls wearing very short shorts. I found an unopened bottle of water in one of the booth cabinets, opened it, and took a swig. I looked back at the phone and picked up the receiver.

"Mr. Trent?" I asked.

"Yes?" He answered.

"I've checked all lost and found entries from two months ago, but I don't see a shirt turned in. I'm very sorry."

"Nobody turned it in? But that was my favorite shirt! I can't believe this! Thank you for checking, though." He said. *His favorite shirt, right*, I thought to myself.

I hung up the phone and went back to watching people. I was musing to myself how funny people were just as a really drunk kid staggered his way to the booth. He grabbed on to the edge of the booth; almost like grabbing onto the edge of a lifeboat, and held himself up as he giggled and smiled at me.

"Hey Man!" he said drunkenly, "I've had a great time here, how do I get copies of the tapes?"

"What tapes?" I asked.

"The tapes, man!" he slurred, "The tapes you people make of us in the casino!"

"I don't have a clue what you're talking about?" I said confused, "Who is making tapes in the casino?"

"You Dudes!" he said, "All the cameras in the casinos watch everybody! How do I get a copy of the tapes of me!"

"So you're telling me the casino has been watching you on the cameras and you want a copy of these tapes; am I right?" I asked.

"There you go!" He yelled. "The tapes!"

"Why was the casino watching you on camera?" I asked.

"Dude, you guys watch everybody! Haven't you seen C.S.I. on TV?"

Once again I felt a strong urge to use two fingers to poke someone in the eyes. "I think I must have missed that episode of C.S.I." I said, "What does TV have to do with what goes on in a real casino?"

"Dude!" he screamed drunkenly, "You guys have got the tapes, I just want a copy because I've had a great time!"

I leaned down near him and tried my best to be nice, "Listen to me, ok? Are you listening to me?" He nodded, "This is *real life*! This is not *C.S.I.* or any other TV show. Just because they showed something on TV doesn't mean it happens in real life, ok? You can't get a copy of any tape from me. Are you understanding what I'm saying to you?"

He looked at me for a second and then nodded. "I know you guys have tapes though, you just don't want me to have them! I probably did something on one."

See you later on in a hallway when we find you passed out with all your

money missing, I thought as he staggered away.

I was never what you would call a "people person," and the people I was

meeting tonight were actually reinforcing those feelings. I actually glanced over

my shoulder at the sign hanging above the booth just to make sure it said

"Security" and not "Idiot Station."

As I turned back around a female porter was standing there holding out a filthy

sneaker. "Shoe." she said.

I looked at the dirty shoe for a minute confused. She repeated herself, "Shoe."

"Yes, shoe." I replied, "And a very filthy shoe at that! Why don't you put that

in the garbage where it belongs?"

"Shoe found." She said and pointed out into the casino.

"Shoe garbage!" I replied and pointed to a nearby trashcan.

She looked confused and rattled off something in Spanish I didn't understand.

Then she spoke some Spanish into a radio she was carrying. A reply came back

over her radio in Spanish. She set the shoe down on the counter in front of me

and started to walk away.

"Hey!" I screamed, "What the hell do you think you're doing? You don't just

leave garbage on my booth!"

She continued to walk away as if not hearing me. *Just another fine person in*

Paradise, I thought to myself. I grabbed a few tissues from a nearby box and just shoved the shoe off the front of the booth. With any luck, Jerry would be back before anyone else would see it and try to give it back to me.

Now the phone began to ring again. I picked it up, "Security Booth, this is Robert."

"Yes, I called about getting some more towels hours ago, and I still haven't gotten any!" Came a female voice.

"I think you want housekeeping." I answered politely.

"I called them for the towels, but they still haven't brought any!" Came the response.

"I understand." I tried, "But you're speaking with the Security Booth, and there's nothing I can do about towels. Let me transfer you."

"Don't transfer….." she started, however I pushed the transfer button, dialed the line for housekeeping and hung up the phone. I smirked a bit at my own efficiency. Another line was ringing, I looked at the caller ID and saw that it was dispatch.

"Booth." I answered simply. I didn't give my name since they had assigned me here for Jerry's lunch, they should know who I was.

"Hey….uh….have you had any ….uh….puppets turned in tonight?" Joey asked.

"Puppets?" I asked. I looked down at the log sheet in front of me, but didn't see a puppet listed. "No, no puppets tonight." I answered.

"Well, if one gets turned in, call me immediately, ok?" Joey said.

"Who's missing a puppet?" I asked, and then it hit me just as Joey answered: "Tom from Jester's Court called and said he was missing a puppet. I guess he left it on a chair backstage and when he went back for it later, it was gone."

"Mr. Funnybuns is missing?" I asked absently.

"Who?" Joey asked.

"Mr. Funnybuns is the name of the puppet, I think." I explained.

"Well, keep an eye out for him and let me know right away if he turns up, ok?" Joey said just before hanging up.

I chuckled to myself. A part of me wondered if Hank had crept into the showroom and removed the puppet during the show. I didn't think he would do that, but people were strange here at the Fabulous Golden Paradise. I knew Hank had been furious when Tom had waved the puppet at him.

While thinking about it, the phone started to ring again. *No rest for the weary,* I thought to myself. "Security Booth, this is Robert." I answered.

"Hi Robert, this is Tom Triphorn from the Jester's Court, how are you tonight?" came a familiar voice. I wondered if he even knew who I was, or would even remember me from the escorts I had done with him.

"I'm fine, Mr. Triphorn. How can I help you tonight?" I said thinking myself extra charming.

"I seem to have misplaced my puppet tonight," he said, "By chance has he been turned in to you?"

"No sir, I'm sorry." I answered, "No puppets turned in tonight. Maybe it'll turn up later. You might want to check back in an hour or so." I fought the urge to tell him that Mr. Funnybuns had been turned in, but had escaped.

"Are you sure?" he asked, "Maybe he's just under something up there?" Tom asked sounding genuinely upset.

Yes Terrible Tom, he is under something up here! And I'm not giving him back! I'm going to fill Mr. Funnybuns full of water and confetti and then send him back to you in a big, wet, burlap sack! This thought raced through my head and I desperately wanted to say it. However, I remained the professional I was supposed to be and instead said, "No, I'm sorry, but nothing has been turned in right now. If the puppet shows up, I'll get word to you right away." I wondered to myself if I was actually telling the truth. Would I get word to him right away?

"Thank you." He said simply and hung up.

On a lark I called the operator, "I'm not sure of the number, can you connect me to the receiving dock, please?" I asked nicely.

The operator put me through and shortly I heard a voice say, "Receiving, this is Barry."

"Hi Barry, this is Robert at the Security Booth. I have a quick question for you: Do you guys have any burlap sacks down there?"

"Sure," answered Barry, "A lot of the fruit and vegetables come in them. Do you need one for something?"

"I might later." I said, "Thanks for the info." I hung up the phone.
This seemed almost like too much fun now. I was ready for the next bizarre person to arrive! I thought to myself how good a TV show the booth would make. People seemed to love reality shows. How about one where we just show on TV what happens at the booth each night! Yahoo! An older lady approached the booth now and looked at me a bit timidly. I looked back at her and smiled, "Hi, I'm Robert. How can I help you tonight?"

"Well," she said, "I know this will sound a bit strange, but I've lost my jeweled lizard."

"That doesn't sound strange to me at all." I smiled, "Strange was the guy who just called me missing his puppet, Mr. Funnybuns. Strange is the guy last week who said he was missing a bag of fish heads. Missing a jeweled lizard doesn't sound strange at all to me." I looked down at the log sheet in front of me and saw a jeweled lizard had been logged in to lost and found by Jerry a couple hours ago.

"Did you say *Mr. Funnybuns*?" the lady asked, "We saw a man with a puppet called Mr. Funnybuns when we were at the comedy show here!"

"That might be the one missing!" I laughed, "Was he at a craps table? He likes to escape now and then and shoot a little bit of craps. We try to discourage him though, because he's only about 2 years old. Gaming violation, you know."

The lady roared into laughter. "That's so cute!"

I opened the lost and found cabinet and located the envelope containing the jeweled lizard. "Is this what you're missing, Ma'am?" I asked as I held it up. "Oh my God, yes!" she screamed, "I can't believe you found it! I was so worried, you've made my night!"

"I was glad to help." I said, "Now I need you to do two things: sign right here for me to show you received back your lost item, and also keep an eye out at those craps tables for Mr. Funnybuns, ok?"

The woman laughed again as she took the pen I offered her. She continued giggling as she signed her name.

"People like you are why I stay here every time I come to Vegas." She smiled.

"Well…." I answered, not really knowing how to reply to that. "Thank you, Ma'am, I'm glad I could make your time here paradise!"

The lady really made me feel good. Praise was hard to come by in the security department. I was so used to being yelled at and sworn at by guests. I almost didn't know how to take any praise.

The rest of the hour went by pretty quickly as I directed guests to the nearest bathroom and answered routine questions. Before I knew it, Jerry was back from lunch.

I left the booth and was pacing around the casino waiting for the shift to end. Tonight had been another busy night for me, and I was ready to go home. I looked at my watch and saw I had just under two hours left. I checked the fill

window several times, but there were no fills. I started to walk towards the

Ambrosia just for the hell of it when Jerry in the booth was calling me:

"Booth to 220." Jerry said over the radio.

"220, go ahead." I answered hoping it was something interesting.

"I need you to swing by, I have a couple things for you." Jerry said.

A couple things for me? I thought. What *things* could he possibly have for

me? I guess there was only one way to find out. I headed to the booth.

As I got near, I saw two women who looked somewhat familiar, but I couldn't

place where I knew them. I got closer and still felt I knew them from somewhere,

but nothing came to me. When I arrived at the booth, Jerry introduced them:

"Ladies, this is Robert. Robert, this is Mrs. Amanda Fletcher and her daughter

Olivia."

"Nice to meet you, ladies." I smiled, "How can I help you tonight?"

"You're the guy that did C.P.R. on my dad last night, right?" Olivia asked.

It all came back to me in a rush: These were the two women with the man I

had done C.P.R. on in the Ambrosia! I hadn't remembered them because Phil had

taken their information and done the report for me! I was quite a bit shook up and

hadn't really talked to them before they left with the paramedics!

"Oh, I'm sorry I didn't recognize you ladies!" I said, "How's he doing? I hope

things turned out ok!"

"You saved his life, and we wanted to say thank you in person." Mrs. Fletcher smiled.

"I saved…." I said confused, once again not used to any kind of praise.
"Yes," Olivia smiled, too, "The doctor said the C.P.R. you did on him saved him and avoided a lot of damage because of how quickly you acted."

I smiled and felt myself blushing a bit. "I just did what anybody would have done." I tried to be modest. A warm and happy feeling flooded through me, though.

Both ladies told me thank you again and each one gave me a hug. I felt like nothing could ruin the rest of my night no matter what.

As the ladies walked off I heard Jerry calling my name, "Robert, what is this here for?"

"What is what for?" I asked. I looked up and saw him holding a burlap sack. It had a small note taped to it with the name *Robert* written on it. I smiled to myself. I reached up and took the sack from Jerry and carried it with me until the end of the shift. You never know when you might need a good burlap sack.

I met up with Matt and Paul to clock out. As we walked to our cars I had a strange, little smile.

"What's the sack for?" Paul asked, "It looks like you have news for us!"

We got to the briefing room and clocked out. Just before walking out I turned and yelled back inside, "Mr. Funnybuns has been kidnapped! They WILL be found, and when they are, buns will roll!"

"Your Funnybuns can kiss my ass!" Hank yelled back from the briefing room.

I started laughing as Paul asked, "Mr. Funnybuns has been what? Who is Mr. Funnybuns?"

I explained everything to him on the way to the cars since he hadn't heard about the lost puppet over the radio. And I hadn't even told him about the escort with Hank the night before. Both Paul and Matt were laughing as we got ready to drive home for the night. Only two more days to go before my days off, and they would both be in dispatch. I sighed to myself as I drove off. Tomorrow the real fun would start.

Chapter Four
Dispatch Phones

I parked my car and headed into the Golden Paradise for work. On my way in I stumbled across Paul. He sauntered up to me as we walked in the employee entrance.

"Hey there, Bobby!" he smiled, "Dispatch tonight?"

"Yup," I sighed, "I guess Matt traded with Joey and we both know he'll want to be on the radio tonight."

"Just tell him no," Paul said as we entered the briefing room, "I know you know that word."

"What do I care?" I answered, "I'll be out there tomorrow too, so I'm sure I'll get my fill of the radio then. Besides, what could be more fun than answering phones and passing calls to an angry, bald man/boy?"

Paul laughed and walked over to his locker. His pre-shift routine was much more complex than mine: gunbelt, keys, gun, vest, SHEESH!! Then he had to walk half way to nowhere to get his bike and bring it all the way back to the briefing room just for the privilege of sitting through a briefing. I walked into the assistant manager's office and saw Walt sitting at his desk.

"Hey Walt," I said cheerfully, "Where's the Master Sheet?"

Walt handed me a paper listing all the officers and their assigned posts for the night. I looked it over while shaking my head. Nothing on that paper looked unusual to me; I just always seemed to shake my head each week when I would work dispatch and get the Master Sheet.

"Get out of my office." Walt said with a smile.

"*Well*!" I said acting indignant, "I've *never* been treated thusly!" I turned around and goose stepped out of the office. I went back into the briefing room and sat down next to Paul. I turned and looked at Paul but didn't say anything. He looked back and after a minute said, "Well, Robert?"

"Well what?" I answered.

"Where's Mathew?" he asked.

"Do I know?" I spouted, "Do I know anything about where this guy is or what he does? Do you somehow think I have any control over this individual?"

Paul smiled at this, "*Roooooobert!*" he drug out my name.

"Ok." I agreed, "Sometimes I suggest he do things he probably shouldn't, but that doesn't mean I know where he is. Keep in mind though, he's no Mr. Funnybuns!" Paul laughed at this. I turned my attention to the front of the room when Walt came out to start tonight's briefing.

"Ok people, settle down and let me have your attention." Walt said, "We need to get things going because we have a lot to go over."

Paul and I looked at each other but didn't say anything. People continued to mill around the room a bit, but finally settled down and the room got quiet for a moment.

"Last night one of the comedians had something of his disappear from...." Walt began. As he was speaking, Matt walked into the briefing room, past Walt, and sat down next to me.

"Nice of you to join us!" Walt growled, "I'm not disturbing you by trying to run a briefing here, am I?"

I started to answer but Paul beat me to it: "You're disturbing me. You shouldn't stop because some slacker came in late."

"Hey, I'm sorry." Matt said, "I overslept. I forgot to set the alarm."

I turned my head to look at Matt and said, "Who the hell *are you*?" Paul let out a slight giggle.

"Are we done back there?" Walt said angrily, "Can I go on with briefing now? Are you people finished?"

With all the other officers looking at us, we realized we were the center of attention. I could tell both Paul and Matt liked that just as much as I did. All three of us mumbled a few things: *"Are you finished? Any more excuses? Anything else to discuss or banter about?"*

Finally Walt had heard enough. "Knock it off back there right now! These briefings are for your benefit! You need to know this stuff and as dispatchers I would think you would take this stuff a bit more seriously! This is my time! Only I talk now!" Walt was turning a bit red.

"Sorry," Paul answered for the three of us, "Please continue with the knowledge!"

Walt glared at him. "As I was saying, one of the comedians from the Jester's Court had some of his property taken last night. We need to keep our eyes open for a puppet that may have been misplaced."

"Misplaced?" I whispered as I glanced sideways at both Matt and Paul.

"This is an important prop and is worth quite a bit of money." Walt continued, "If located, you need to notify a manager immediately."

Not being able to resist the urge, I raised my hand and asked, "How much is this *prop* supposed to be worth?"

"The memo I have says the value is approximately ten thousand dollars." Walt answered.

"Ten *thousand*?" I snickered, "Have you *seen* this puppet?" I asked.

"Hey," Walt answered, "I didn't give the value, the owner did. We just need to keep an eye out for the puppet, ok?"

"Is there a reward for this mega puppet?" I continued pestering Walt.

"Don't you mean a ransom?" Paul asked and I burst out laughing.

"I'll need to see you three after briefing." Walt scowled.

"What did I do?" Matt began whining.

"Continuing on," Walt tried, "We still need to continue recommending the Jester's Court to each guest we speak with. You should also be recommending the hotel's restaurants as places to eat."

"Now we're shills." I whispered to Matt.

"Outside units," Walt announced, "I guess we are having problems with employees trying to valet their cars. This will stop. I know none of us would do that, but if you see someone from another department trying to valet their car, you need to notify management immediately."

I raised my hand again, "Shouldn't the valets be telling the employees no and then notifying management themselves?"

"Can I go over the memos, please?" Walt shot back, "These get passed to me and I pass them on to you. Apparently the valets are parking the employee cars and if you see this you need to notify a manager, ok?"

"Fabulous." I answered back.

Walt went over a few more things, but I wasn't really listening. I was hoping he'd finish quickly, yell at Matt, Paul, and me and then let us leave. He went on for a few more minutes and finally ended with, "Ok, let's have a safe night."

The other officers filed out of the office. The three of us strolled into Walt's office.

"Yell away." I said.

"Yell?" Walt said confused, "What do you want me to yell at you for?"

I looked at Paul and then Matt. "You said you wanted to see us three after briefing."

"Ah, yes." Walt said nicely, "Do any of you guys know anything about this missing puppet?"

"Why would we know anything about it?" Paul asked

"It's just a question." Walt answered, "I heard there was a bit of a problem the other night when Hank was upstairs doing the entertainer escort. I just thought you guys might have heard something."

"If there was a bit of a problem with Hank, shouldn't you be talking to Hank right now?" Paul asked.

"So Walt, you suspect Hank of unsavory behavior?" I smirked, "Or do you think we strung up Mr. Funnybuns from a flag pole on the top floor?"

"Who?" Walt said confused.

"Mr. Funnybuns is the name of the missing puppet." I answered. "Didn't anybody tell you anything about this?"

"No." Walt said, "I had a note on my desk that said to ask around about it. You three usually know what's going on around here so I thought you could shed some light on what this is all about."

"Well, let me tell you a bit about our comedian," I said, "and that might help out a bit. Tom Triphorn is a major prick. When we do his escort to the theater he occasionally likes to hit officers in the head with confetti, or squirt us with water.

We know what he's like. That's why only a few of us will do the escort.

Recently he added a puppet to his act called Mr. Funnybuns. It's a dime store toy,

maybe worth two bucks, not ten thousand. So you're probably being told to ask
around because I would guess somebody thinks some unhappy officer might have

swiped the puppet."

"He does *what* to the officers who escort him?" Walt asked, genuinely

surprised.

"He throws confetti and squirts water at us." Matt answered. "We know the

drill."

"He doesn't have a right to treat officers like that!" Walt said mad now, "Why

wasn't I notified about this?"

"It's not as bad as it sounds Walt," I said, "He just screws around a bit and

usually it's a laugh to escort him. He doesn't hit you hard. If you can take a joke,

it's not so bad! They give us free tickets to shows if we ask. We can also get

drinks and snacks out of the green room in the Court and meet all the people

performing, so we put up with it."

"And now someone who didn't think it was very funny took his puppet?" Walt

asked.

"We don't know!" I answered, "He called me at the booth last night and said it

was missing. It disappeared last night during a show, I think."

"So as far as we know, none of the officers took the puppet, though?" Walt asked.

"As far as *we know*," Paul answered, "The puppet walked off on its own."

Walt looked at the three of us for a minute and said, "Ok guys, thanks for the info. Head out to your posts. If you do find out anything about the puppet, let me know please, ok?"

"You mean after we take it down from the flagpole on the top floor?" I asked, "Just kidding, Walt! Geez, don't look so serious!"

I noticed Walt scowling at me as we walked out of the office. I wondered if he believed us, or if he actually thought we might have had something to do with the puppet's disappearance.

Mathew and I left Paul and walked down the hall to dispatch. I used my key and we walked in on the two guys we would be relieving.

"Are we having fun in here?" I joked as we entered.

"These fucking phones will *not stop ringing!*" one said as he looked up angrily. As if to show me, right on cue, the phone started to ring again.

"Busy night." I said as I looked at Matthew. He gave me a sarcastic smile in return.

I searched around the small room, found a vacant chair, and sat down. Matthew walked back out into the hallway for a quick smoke before we got started. I chuckled as I watched the other dispatcher screaming into the phone. A shift in dispatch could really make you tense some days.

"I *told you*," he yelled, "I'll get someone there as soon as I can!" He turned to me, "Do you guys have someone to send to the Box Café? They won't leave me alone about some guy sleeping there!"

"Send 501, Cortez." I answered.

The officer on the radio began calling Cortez. I leaned back in the chair and listened as Cortez had to be called four times before answering his radio.

"Is there something *wrong* with him?" the radio guy asked me.

I nodded, "Yes, there is. You guys seem a bit stressed, so feel free to head out whenever you're ready." They were both getting up out of their chairs before I even finished the sentence. I moved over to the chair near the phone just as a line lit up and the phone began to ring. "Security, this is Robert." I answered nicely.

"You have a sleepy in da over on....yes, over in de sleepy." A voice said with a thick accent.

I looked down at the caller ID on the phone to see where the call was coming from. It was from a maid's closet in the main tower, but didn't specify what floor.

"What's going on?" I asked, "You're really sleepy?"

"No!" the voice answered, "Dey sleepy in da room! Dey sleepy in da room!"

"They're sleepy in the room." I repeated, "You should probably suggest a nap then."

"*Yes!*" came the voice, "Day nappin! Dey nappin in de room!"

"Outstanding!" I said, "Let's not disturb them and hope they have sweet dreams!" I hung up the phone. More than likely the person was calling about someone passed out in a hallway somewhere, but with English that bad, I didn't have time to try and figure out where it was.

Matthew entered as I was hanging up. "So what are we on so far?" he asked.

"Cortez is pretending to deal with a sleeper at the Box. That should be it!" I smiled.

Now two different lines began ringing on the phone. I picked up one, and Matthew answered the other using the phone on his side of the radio terminal.

"Security, this is Robert." I said again as pleasantly as I could.

"Dude, I want to go to my damned room!" someone screamed drunkenly into the phone.

"Fabulous," I answered, "Feel free to do so."

"Where is it?" he screamed.

"Where is what?"

"Where's my room? Are you *fucking stupid*!" the person screamed into the phone.

"I don't know." I answered, "That's quite an interesting question, let me ask my supervisor. Please hold." I pushed the hold button and set the receiver back in the phone cradle. I watched the light on the phone, waiting for it to go out when he hung up. It stayed lit. He was actually waiting on hold for me to ask my supervisor if I was fucking stupid. Lovely. Another line began to ring and I answered that.

"Security, this is Robert."
"Yes, this is Jody in the poker room," came a female voice, "We have a guy over here claiming he's secret service."

"I see," I said, "Does he need some kind of security assistance?"

"I don't think so," Jody answered, "But I just thought you guys should know about it."

"You thought we should know about a guy is claiming to be secret service." I repeated back blandly, "Has he shown you a badge or any kind of ID?"

"Uh, no."

"Is he bothering any other guests or employees or flashing a firearm?"

"No, I just thought…."

"I see," I said grumpily, "Thank you for calling, have a nice night." I hung up.

I looked over at Matt who was still chatting on the phone with someone. He hung up and looked over at me and then back at the phone. "Oh, is this one for me?" he asked and answered the line on hold.

I just watched. "Security, this is Matt. How can I help you? What? No, I don't know why you were on hold so long sir, just a minute." He looked over at me for an explanation.

"He was on hold waiting for me to call my supervisor and ask if I'm fucking stupid." I explained.

Matt turned back towards the monitors in front of us. "Sir? Yes, I believe I do have an answer for you, he's not fucking stupid. Have a great time in Paradise!" He hung up and looked at me. "There, you didn't need to ask a supervisor after all!"

We sat quietly for a few minutes looking at the monitors in front of us. Finally, I broke the silence: "What do you suppose really happened to Mr. Funnybuns?"

"I don't know," Matt answered, "I never even got to see the puppet. It must be something pretty new from the other night. I do wonder why all of a sudden it's getting made into such a big deal."

"Hank was pretty mad the other night; you know how serious he takes security sometimes. Do you think he went into the theater and took the puppet?"

The phone rang. "Hold that thought, Matt. Security this is Robert." I answered.

"Yeah Robert, this is Jenny in the Café, are you guys sending someone for this guy sleeping in the booth?"

I looked over at Matt, "We sent somebody 20 minutes ago, and he isn't there yet?"

"Ah no, no one's come. We need this guy to leave, we really need the booth."

"Don't worry," I said, "I'll make sure someone gets over there post haste." I hung up the phone and looked over at Matt. "They sent Cortez to the café to wake up a sleeper just before we took over and he hasn't bothered to show up."

Matt turned angrily towards the radio in front of him, "Control to 501!"

After a short delay, "501, go!"
"Why aren't you at the café waking up the sleeper like you were dispatched to

do 20 minutes ago?" Matt growled.

"I'm almost there," Cortez answered, "Just about there now."

"I don't believe this!" Matt screamed at me, "Does anybody besides us

actually do any work here?"

I looked at Matt curiously. "Forget that, do you think Hank could have taken

the puppet?"

"I'm not going to forget it! He needs to be doing what he's dispatched to do!

He can't just *not do things*!" Matt continued to scream.

"Oh for crying out loud!" I screamed back, "He always acts like this, why are

you so surprised? Just let it go and let's get back to the puppet!"

"I don't care about the stupid puppet!" Matt said as he turned towards the

monitors and began to pout.

I went back to looking at the monitors. I watched a few people amble through

the casino stopping to drop a dollar here and there into slot machines. I leaned

over and used the control to zoom in and watch a young man. He was at the main

entrance and puking in a garbage can. After watching him for a minute, he didn't

stand back up.

"Hey Matt," I said, "Looks like we have a guy sleeping in the garbage can at the entrance."

I was watching you zoom in on him." Matt smiled, "I'll send Phil."
I zoomed the camera in a bit more, "You can send Cortez after he finishes with his sleeper in the café. Of course that might be another 7 hours."

Instead, Matt sent Phil. We watched as Phil went over and began to talk to the guy. Slowly he got the man to pull his head out of the garbage can and walk over to sit on a bench. I could picture myself just grabbing the man by the belt and pulling him out of the can roughly until he fell on the floor. Instead, I thought, it was much better for me to answer the phones in dispatch and have Phil deal with the drunken man.

"501 to Control?" Cortez called, and I instantly lost interest in the garbage can drunk.

"Go ahead 501." Matt answered.

"501 to Control?" Cortez called again.

"I said *go ahead!*" Matt said angrily.

"This guy fell asleep while he was eating, but I woke him up. He's going to pay his bill and go back up to his room. He's from California and said he's just a little bit drunk. He doesn't want to cause us…."

I began laughing so hard I didn't hear the rest of what Cortez said. His radio transmission seemed to go on forever! Part way through it I found myself pounding on my radio trying to talk over him; however the equipment wouldn't let me. I turned to Matt and began to spout loud gibberish, "Momomo, gigigigi, fofofofo!" and then continued to laugh!

Matt wasn't laughing and just looked mad. "What the hell is the matter with these people? They don't show up to calls, but when they do they have to tell me some drunken sleeper's life story?"

"Who are *These people*?" I immediately shot back, "It's only Cortez doing that so far!"

"This is why I don't like to be out here!" Matt grumbled.

"You *traded* to be out here!" I began to laugh, "If you don't like it, why would you trade for this?"

"Well, we always have fun!" he said as he turned to look at me.

"You still haven't told me who *these people* are." I said, still giggling.

The phone began to ring again. The caller ID displayed a bunch of ones. This meant it was a police emergency dispatcher.

"Security, this is Robert." I answered pleasantly.

"Hi Robert, this is Metro Police dispatch calling. How are you doing tonight?" a female voice said.

"Fine," I replied, "How can I help you tonight, Officer?"

"We have an officer on the way concerning some property stolen from one of your theaters." She said, "The call came from a Mr. Triphorn."

"Mr. Funnybuns again." I said almost to myself, "You're sending an officer for this?"

"Yes we are and he should be at the hotel shortly. Do you know anything about this theft?" she asked.

I looked over at Matt who was watching me curiously. "Just the basics. He's our resident comedian and host at the Jester's Court. He recently lost a puppet named Mr. Funnybuns."

"I see…." The officer said sounding a bit skeptical, "When the officer gets there could you maybe fill him in a bit on all this?"

"Not a problem." I answered, "If you can, just have him pull right up to the front entrance and I'll send an officer out to meet him."

"Ok," she said sounding happy for the assistance, "Have a good night and stay safe!" and she hung up.

I hung up the phone and looked at Matt with a smile on my face. "What is it?" he asked after a minute.

"You know….." I began, "Someone should really write a book about this place! I swear this is straight out of Wonderland! Send someone out front to meet a Metro Officer; he's coming in to investigate the missing Mr. Funnybuns."

"Oh you *are* kidding me, aren't you?" Matt asked me. I shook my head. "Cortez should be free, I'll send him."

"Oh yeah, great idea" I said, "It should only take him a few hours to find the main entrance."

Matt chuckled and called Cortez on the radio. No answer. He tried again and still didn't receive an answer. You could hear Matt's anger go out over the radio the third time he tried to reach Cortez.

"Bike 3, go ahead." came Paul's voice.

Before Matt could answer him or get mad I pressed my radio button, "Bike three log off track and meet up with Metro at the Main Entrance, please. Escort him where ever he needs to go."

I looked over at Matt, "Take him off track, he should *love* this!"

Right away another phone line started ringing. I could see it was the line from Stan's office. "Hi Boss," I said as I picked up the phone, "I was just about to call you.

"Let's hear it, fill me in." Stan said.

"Metro called, they're sending an officer to investigate this missing puppet. We're just going to assist him and take him where ever he needs to go."

"Why are you sending a bike unit?" Stan asked, "Send an inside unit for this."

"We were trying to call Cortez, but he doesn't answer." I replied.

"Then either keep trying or call someone else. You know the bikes stay outside."

"Yeah, ok. I'll pass it on to Matt." I smiled into the phone and hung up. "Stan won't let us send Paul, dispatch somebody else."

Matt tried to call Cortez a fourth time and finally got an answer.

"501, go ahead!" came a sleepy sounding voice.

"Meet up with Metro at the main entrance and escort them around!" Matt shouted into the radio angrily.

I leaned back in my chair and wondered what had actually happened to the puppet. I looked over at Matt who was still sulking. "Want to see something new?" I asked.

Matt looked over at me as I started punching a couple of numbers into the camera keyboard control. A picture popped up near a back area of the pool. I looked up at the monitor and saw Cortez standing right in front of the camera with another officer named Walter. "What the hell?" I asked myself.

"Hey, that's behind the pool shack!" Matt said surprised, "How'd you know Cortez was out there? And when did we get this camera?"

"They just put the camera up a couple days ago. I kept complaining about officers hiding to smoke out there." I answered, "I didn't know Cortez was hiding there now, though. I guess that explains why he never answered you."

Matt reached for the radio button. I quickly reached over and stopped him. "Whoa there, if you let them know we finally have a camera up, they won't hide there anymore. Let it go for a few days before you start screaming at people, ok?"

Matt scowled over at me. "We should still tell Stan about this."

"Whatever." I mumbled and walked over to the dispatch door. "I'm going to take a quick pee, I'll be right back." I left dispatch and walked down the hall to

the nearest restroom. This was still in the basement and so still just an employee

area. I watched a cocktail waitress walking down the hall toward me. I paused
outside the bathroom door to let her get a little bit closer. Once she got close I let

out a loud fart. I walked into the bathroom quickly enjoying the foul look she had

given me.

After doing my business, I walked back to dispatch. I entered and sat down,

Matt said, "Your new friend called for you."

"My new friend?" I asked.

"You know," he smiled, "Chef Boy-R-Dee!"

"Chef…." I said confused, "Oh, you mean *Henry*! What did he want?"

"He wanted you to come to the Ambrosia. I tried to tell him you were out here

tonight and couldn't come, but he just kept yelling that you needed to come and

then hung up."

"Yeah, that sure sounds like Chef Henry." I said, "I'm sure he'll call back

later."

I looked at the monitor showing the front of the hotel and saw Paul talking to a

young police officer. "When did Metro get here?" I asked, "And where is

Cortez?"

Before Matt could answer, Paul came over the radio, "Bike Three to Control,

Metro would like to speak with you guys. Since Cortez can't find his way out here, I'll bring him down to dispatch."

"Copy, Bike Three." Matt replied. "Why would he want to talk to us?" he

asked me.

"Maybe Ol' Terrible told him Security stole his puppet." I replied. "Who

knows? We'll find out when he gets here."

We sat in silence for a few minutes. Pretty soon Paul and the police officer

came into dispatch.

Both Matt and I greeted the policeman and asked if he wanted to sit down. He

shook his head and pulled out a little notebook. He introduced himself as Officer

Broderick and started asking us a few questions: "So what can you guys tell me

about this puppet?"

"Not much," I answered, "I only saw it once while escorting him down to the

theater."

"So you just saw it with the victim, right? Was anyone else with you when you

last saw the puppet?"

"Yeah," I said cautiously, "I was training another officer to do the escort. He

was a bit…..upset during the escort."

"Who were you training? Officer Broderick asked.

"Uh…..you really aren't doing a big investigation into a missing puppet, are

you?" I asked a bit shocked.

"Well because of the value given for the puppet, we have to look into this.

He's filed a police report. So who was it you were training and why was he a bit upset?" he asked.

The phone started to ring and for once I was glad to answer it. This puppet thing seemed to be getting more and stranger all the time.

"Security, this is Robert."

"Uh…..yeah, Robert, this is Stewart." came a droning voice, "I'm outside the, uh, 8 Star club and, uh, the guy here with me, uh, his girlfriend needs the paramedics."

"You're with a guy whose girlfriend needs the paramedics? Where's his girlfriend now?" I asked.

"Yeah, uh, he doesn't know." came the answer.

"He doesn't know? She needs the paramedics, but he doesn't know where she is. Is that correct?" I asked.

"Yeah, uh, I guess he drugged her, and now he, uh, doesn't know where she is." Stewart said.

"He's telling you he drugged her?" I asked stunned, "He's admitting to a crime, but doesn't know where the person he committed the crime against is?"

"Well, she uh, needs the paramedics." Stewart continued, "He put a lot of uh, stuff in her, uh, drink and thinks he might have, uh, used too much."

I pulled the phone away from my ear and looked at Matt, and then Officer Broderick. I opened my mouth, but couldn't think of anything to say. I put the phone back up to my ear, "Where is this girl now?"

"He, uh, doesn't know. But, uh, she needs the, uh, paramedics. See, uh, he put

a lot of stuff in her, uh, drink." Stewart droned onward.
"Yeah, I get all that." I said, "Once more, *where is his girlfriend?*"

"Uh…..he, uh, doesn't know, but she needs the….."

I cut him off in mid sentence, "If you don't even know where she is, how could

I bring the paramedics to her?" I asked.

"Oh, now that you, uh, say that, I uh, guess you're, uh, right about that."

Stewart said seeming to confuse himself even more than normal.

"Find this girl and then get back to me, ok?" I instructed him and hung up the

phone.

"What was that?" Matt asked.

"Stewart has a guy with him who says he put too many drugs in his girlfriend's

drink and wants the paramedics. Neither the guy nor Stewart knows where the

girl is right now." I answered.

"He's admitting to drugging a woman?" Officer Broderick asked.

"Yes, he has!" I said happily, "Welcome to Paradise! Would you like to go

and have a talk with him? He doesn't know where the victim is, though."

"Not without a victim, no." he answered, "But if you do find her and she is

drugged, let me know. Back to whom you were training?"

"Right," I said "Whom I was training. We teach each other about things up there like the doorbell outside the room. It squirts water. We let the officers who

haven't done the escort before know that he throws confetti, or might squirt you

with water, but he's harmless. It's just like escorting a jacked up Rip Taylor, only
we don't think he's that funny. Anyway, I was training a guy named *Hank*."

Broderick wrote something in his little notebook and then asked, "And what

was Hank upset about? He didn't like how Mr. Triphorn was acting, right?"

"Well, if I remember right, he walked over to Hank and Hank grabbed the

puppet and threw it in a corner. He was bit pissed off that Tom wouldn't leave

and let us start the escort. Maybe the puppet's still in the corner?"

"I'll make sure I take a look." Broderick said, "Was this last night?"

"Uh, no." I said thinking back, "It was on my second night of work so that

would make it Thursday night."

"So when was the first time you knew the puppet was missing?" he asked me.

"I don't know." I answered, "I guess that would be last night when Tom called

me while I was at the booth to see if it had been turned in to lost and found."

"And I'm guessing it wasn't?" he asked.

I shook my head. I looked over at Matt who was just watching me talk. "Feel

free to chime in here anytime!" I said nastily.

"I never got to see the puppet!" Matt laughed, "I don't know *anything* about

it!"

The phone began to ring again, "Security, this is Robert."

"Hey, uh, Robert! This is Stewart again!" came the annoying voice, "I think we found the uh, girl! I, uh, we, uh, think she's, uh, in the 8 Star!"

"So bring her out." I said angrily.
"Well, uh, we think she's still, uh, in there, but we're not, uh…..sure." Stewart droned onward.

An image flashed through my mind of placing a shock collar on Stewart that would give him a jolt every time he said the word "*uh.*"

"Why are you calling me if you aren't sure?" I asked, "If she's in there, bring her out and call me back! If she can't come out because she's incapacitated let me know and I'll roll the paramedics in there. But don't call me because you think she *might* be somewhere! Use your head!" I growled.

"Oh, uh." Stewart began again, "I just wanted you to, uh; know we were, uh, still looking, ok?"

"Yeah, right!" I said and hung up the phone.

I looked back at Officer Broderick, "Tom would probably be more helpful than I am. Would you like us to take you up to his room?"

"You've been pretty helpful, so don't think you haven't!" the Officer said nicely, "But yes, I'd like to talk to Mr. Triphorn and see the room if I could?"

I looked at both Paul and Matt, "Where's Cortez? I thought he was supposed to be doing this escort?"

"Control to 501?" Matt called into the radio.

"I'm almost at the Main Entrance now!" came Cortez's voice.

"It's been like 20 minutes since I called him!" Matt screamed, "Control to 501, meet the officer at dispatch now."
"Copy." Came the dull reply.

We waited another ten minutes before Cortez finally showed up at dispatch. No explanation of where he had been or why it had taken so long for him to find the police officer. He just walked into dispatch as if it was no big deal to be late. He looked around nervously at Paul, Matt, and me.

"So where am I taking him now?" Cortez asked.

All three of us glared at him. Finally Officer Broderick spoke up, "I need to see Tom Triphorn, please."

Cortez looked around, "Where's he at?"

"Probably in his room." I said after a few seconds of silence.

"Ohhhhh," Cortez said as if just remembering, "And where's his room?"

"Maybe you better call Jack or someone else who can handle this?" I said to Matt.

"No, no!" Cortez piped up, "I can do this! I just don't know what room this Mr. Triphorn is in."

I looked at Paul and Matt and then glared at Cortez again, "52100. The same room we do the Jester's escort from every time there's a show."

"Hey," Cortez said brightly, "That's the same room where that comedian lives!"

"What a shocker, huh?" I replied back brightly.

Cortez and Officer Broderick walked out the dispatch door and Paul took a seat. "Well ladies, I think it's time for me to take a personal!"

Before I could reply the phone rang again. I looked at the caller ID and saw it was a phone near the 8 Star Club.

"That's probably Stewart again and I'm done with him." I said as the phone continued to ring. "No more, I've heard enough *uh's* for my entire *week*!"

"Oh, let me!" Paul said as he moved over towards my phone, "Security, this is Paul!"

I watched Paul as he listened to whatever was being said on the phone. For a minute a look of frustration came over his face as if he was listening to some foreign language. Finally he said, "Why are you telling me someone *doesn't* need the paramedics? There are thousands of people here tonight who don't need paramedics. Ok, listen to what I'm saying! Stop talking! Stop....Look; I said to stop talk....." Paul just hung up the phone.

"Did he stop talking?" I asked.

"I doubt it." Paul answered, "He kept going on and on about finding some girl who didn't need the paramedics. I kept telling him to stop talking, but he just kept talking over me going on and on!"

"Isn't dispatch fun?" I asked as the phone rang again. "Security, this is

Robert." I listened carefully to a man tell me he was locked out of his room. I asked his name, checked the name on the computer in front of me, and then turned to pass the call to Matt.

"Guest lockout," I said, "21123, Mr. Butt."

Matt repeated the number and then looked up at me, "Mr. Butt? This is a joke, right?"

"No," I said seriously, "Guest lockout, 21123 Mr. Butt."

"Is it Mr. Funnybutt?" Paul asked laughing.

"Cousin to Mr. Funnybuns, right?" I said also laughing, "He's here to help Mr. Funnybuns get out of the country." Both Paul and I roared with laughter. I looked over at Matt, "That really is a call, though."

Matt turned to the radio and put out the call, "Control to 268, guest lockout at 21123. Last of....." Matt looked over at me, "Butt."

268 was Shirly. "What was that last name again?" she asked.

"Last of Butt." Matt repeated.

"This is just turning into a *Butt* of a night, isn't it?" Paul asked.

"You mean a *Funnybutt of a night*?" I asked and we both roared with laughter again.

So far it had been a pretty quiet night except for the police looking for Mr. Funnybuns. Paul finished his personal and went back outside to his bike patrol. I looked over at Matt who was staring at one of the monitors.

"278 to Control?" the radio crackled to life.

"Go ahead 278." Matt answered.

This was Walter, the guy we had seen earlier outside with Cortez. "Yeah, 278 to Control I have a guy here who doesn't know what room he's in."

Matt looked over at me as it would be my job for the night to not only answer the phones, but also to take care of looking things up on the computer, such as in what room a guest was staying. "Go ahead with his name, 278." I said into the radio.

"Ah, he's staying with a Ned." Walter said sounding a bit confused.

I looked at Matt. "I don't really care who he's staying with, what is his name?"

"He's not registered to the hotel, but he is staying here with Ned. They're both from California." Walter continued.

I looked up at the monitors in front of me as if they could give me a bit of help, then said into the radio, "I can't give you someone else's room number, I can only look up info for the guy you have with you. You should know that!"

"Yeah, but he's staying with Ned." Walter said again.

"Ned who?" I asked starting to get aggravated.

"Ned; Ned from California." Walter answered. "He says there's a one somewhere in the room number, if that helps."

"Take him to the Front Desk." I said into the radio, "There's nothing we can do for him if he's not registered to the hotel."

"But he's not registered," Walter continued, "And he's staying with Ned. The Front Desk said they won't help him."

I turned to Matt, "He's not really this dumb, is he? This has to be some kind of act!"

"He's staying with NED!" Paul's voice came over the radio, "You know, Ned! Ned from California!"

"And there's a one in the room number!" Walter added, as if Paul was helping and not making fun of him.

I leaned back in my chair and the phone began to ring. "Security, this is Robert."

"I've lost my shoes!" Came a slurred voice.

"Well, that's what happens when you bet too much." I answered without missing a beat.

"No, no! I've lost my SHOES!" the voice said again, only louder.

I looked over at Matt, "He's lost his SHOES!" I repeated. I pushed the transfer button and sent the call to the Security booth for lost and found just as the phone began to ring again.

"Security, this is Robert." I quickly answered.

"Hi Robert, this is Metro Police. How is your night going?" Said a calm voice.

"Well, I think I'm in Wonderland." I answered, "Are you going to make my life a bit more exciting now?"

"Probably," the officer said, "We have a report of an armed robbery in your parking garage. Units are on the way right now, can you have someone respond and check it out?"

"Oh shit!" I said, "Do we know where this is taking place, what part of the garage?"

"Sorry, no." came the reply, "This is from a 911 call and the only location they gave before hanging up was Golden Paradise Parking."

"Ok, I'll notify our outside units and call you back if we find out anything new before your units arrive, ok?" I said.

"Thank you Robert that will help a lot." she said and hung up the phone.

I turned to Matt, "Armed robbery somewhere in the garage, unknown area. Have the outside units check around and I'll notify Stan."

Matt put out the call on the radio and I called Stan to update him. We began to search around on the cameras mounted around in the parking garage to see if we could find anything going on at the moment. Suddenly, there was quick movement as we were moving a camera around.

"Move it back!" I screamed at Matt.

"Yeah, I saw it, too!" Matt said as he panned back towards the movement. We saw a young, black kid running through the garage. "Keep on him!" Matt yelled as he quickly punched the radio and put out the man's description and the direction he was running.

"Oh shit!!" I yelled, almost to myself as Jack ran by the camera.

Matt looked up and saw Jack running behind the black kid. "ALL UNITS, DO NOT APPROACH THE SUSPECT!" he screamed into the radio, "HE'S POSSIBLY ARMED, DO NOT APPROACH HIM!"

Jack continued to chase the suspect. We watched as the black kid reached into his shirt while running and pulled out a small gun. He turned and fired a shot at Jack. Jack paused for a few seconds and appeared to think about what he was doing. Then he began the chase again. I sat staring at the monitor, horrified.

After a few seconds I leaned across to the radio and yelled, "Jack, what is the matter with you? You're going to get yourself killed! Back off!"

Jack didn't show any sign of even hearing me. I was about to yell at him to back off again, but several police cruisers pulled up and cut off the kid's escape. Police officers jumped out of the cars and grabbed the kid just as Jack ran up and began pointing and screaming something. I wished the monitors had sound. The phone rang and I could see the call was coming from Stan's office.

"Security, this is Robert." I answered while still staring at the monitor.

"What the hell is going on?" came Stan's voice, "Who is approaching the suspect?"

"Well," I answered, "Metro's got him now, but he took a shot at Jack while Jack was chasing him."

"He WHAT?" Stan screamed.

"He took a shot at Jack." I repeated, "They're all out in front of the hotel now, cops, suspect and Jack." Stan hung up the phone and I knew he was on his way outside. I wondered to myself what he was going to say to Jack. Maybe Stan needed some liver to hit him with?

On the monitor we could see three bike officers in a little group standing near the police cruisers. I knew Paul would be one of them; he was always on the job for emergencies.

I reached for the radio, "Control to Bike Three."

"Bike Three, go ahead, Sir." Paul answered.

"I see the suspect in custody, but where is the victim?" I asked.

"I don't know. Who put out the call?" Paul asked.

"The call came from Metro dispatch, and they got it from a 911 call. Can you check the garage for me and see if there's a victim in there somewhere? Start with the ground floor, that's where we picked up the chase."

"Ground floor, copy." Paul answered and he rode off towards the garage. Paul met with the other two bikes. Paul coordinated the check of the rest of the garage. I saw him doing this on camera and he gave me the thumbs up. I understood his signal and acknowledged him by saying, "Copy Bike 3, keep me updated."

Matt looked over at me, "That guy shot at Jack!"

I started to laugh, "I saw that! Any idea why Jack didn't draw his weapon and fire back?"

"Bike Three on two." Came Paul's voice over the radio's channel two. This channel was usually used when you didn't want everyone to hear what you were saying.

"Go ahead on two." Matt answered.

"What is Jack doing outside? And was he really shot at before we got on scene?" Paul asked.

"Apparently," Matt started, "He ran outside to be shot at."

"Lead One to Control." Came Stan's voice over channel one.

"Go ahead Lead One." Matt answered.

"Find the phone number for the Chief and give him a call. Let him know we have a suspected armed robbery and one of our units was fired on, ok?" Stan said calmly.

"Copy, Sir, calling now." Matt answered as he looked over at me.

"Why do I have to call?" I moaned, "You traded to be out here!"

"You're on the phone side." He answered with a smile.

I never liked calling the chief for anything. We had to notify him for any emergency, or anything major that happened at the Golden Paradise. He wouldn't like hearing that someone had shot at an officer. I found the number and dialed the phone.

"278 to Control." Came Walter's voice, "Did you find this guy's room yet? Where Ned is staying?"

I looked over at Matt, "Do you believe this idiot?" Mr. Landau the Chief answered his phone. "Good evening, Sir." I said thinking he must be really pissed off to be called at home. "This is Robert at the Golden Paradise dispatch. We've had a suspected armed robbery and the suspect fired a weapon at one of our officers."

"I see," said Mr. Landau, "Is he alright, was anybody hit? Were any shots fired by our people?" His questions were coming fast now.

"No to all three questions, Sir." I answered, "Metro has the suspect right now. Everything is calm at the moment."

"Ok, Robert." Mr. Landau said, "Let your supervisors know I'll be coming in shortly. Call my cell phone if anything changes, ok?"

"Ok, Sir." I said, "See you in a bit." I hung up the phone as Matt was once again telling Walter to take Ned's friend to the front desk.

A short time later Paul was calling in and telling us there was no victim in the parking garage. He and the other two bike units had searched the entire garage, and the few people they did come across said they didn't know anything at all about a robbery. This just piled on the problems.

Another phone call, "Security, this is Robert." I answered.

"*Robair!*" Came a familiar voice, "Zis is you? Why are you out zere? I need you to assist me at ze Ambrosia!"

"Henry?" I asked surprised, "What do you need? Tell me what's going on and

I'll send somebody."

"You are ze one who assists me!" shouted Henry, "Can you come out from ze dispatch?"

"Henry…." I started, "Look, I can't leave dispatch, and even if I could, I can't tonight we're too busy out here. Just tell me what you need and I'll send someone who can help, ok?"

"You cannot leave?" Henry asked, "You vill get lunch, yes?"

"Nope," I answered, "We're usually too busy to get a lunch down here. I'll be fine though, what's going on that you need assistance with?"

"Zat is not fair!" Henry screamed, "You vill get ze lunch tonight!" and he hung up the phone.

"Oh for crying out loud!" I said to myself as I hung up the phone, "Hey Matt, send somebody over to the Ambrosia and see what the hell is going on."

"Who was that one the phone?" he asked.

"Henry." I said, "Wanting me to come to the Ambrosia again. He always calls for me now! What a pain in the ass!"

Matt sent Phil over to see what was going on at the Ambrosia. We turned back to the monitor to watch the police who were still out front now talking to Stan.

"Lead One on two." Stan said over channel two.

"Go ahead on two." Matt answered.

"You guys got the suspect on camera firing the weapon, correct? Can you roll up that footage and I'll bring in the Detective to look at it?"

"Affirm, Sir." Matt answered, "We did get it and we'll roll it up for you right now." He looked over at me.

"Lovely." I said, "Just lovely. If opportunity calls for me, you'll tell him I'm busy, right?"

Matt laughed and I headed into a back room of dispatch. There was a computer located there used to look up what the dispatch cameras recorded. Everything was on several hard drives now and it wouldn't take me long to find the footage.

Just as I found the video of the guy shooting at Jack I heard Matt yell from the other room, "Hey Robert! One of the cooks threw some macaroni salad!"

I stepped back into the dispatch room with Matt, "What? What the hell are you talking about?"

"Phil called me just a minute ago." Matt explained, "Henry was mad because one of the cooks was screwing around and threw some macaroni salad at another cook."

"And he wanted me to do what?" I asked, "Show up and start slapping people with liver? Am I the Liver Avenger now? What the hell was I supposed to do, yell at these guys after he did?"

Matt started laughing and began to sing, "Macaroni went to town, riding on a pony, stuck macaroni in its hat and called it macaroni!"

"You profane all of America with that horrible parody." I said just as Stan opened the door to dispatch.

Stan and the Detective came in and watched the footage. They watched it several times and then the questions started.

"Did you see where the bullet went?" the Sergeant asked, "Did it hit a car or anything like that?"

"I don't know." I said, "We were just trying to keep the suspect on camera. So far, we can't even find the robbery victim."

"Nobody was located?" Stan asked.

"Nope," I said, "All we have for now is the call from Metro Dispatch, and Jack on film being fired on. I don't even know why he was chasing the guy. Did Jack say where the victim was?"

"Jack says he went out into the garage, saw the suspect and when he screamed at him the guy started to run away." Stan explained, "He says he didn't see a victim either."

"So he saw a black guy in the garage and started to scream at him and then chased him?" I asked.

"Let it go." Stan said with a stern look.

"We're going to have to shut down that part of the garage for now." the Detective said, "We'll have to try and find the bullet, so it's a crime scene."

"Ok," I said feeling tired already, "Is there any way we can assist you with this?"

"If you could," the Detective asked, "Can you post officers at all entrances and exits to the garage? We can't let anybody in or out for now."

"You got it." I said, "Maaaaaaaathew!" I sang as I walked back into the main part of dispatch, "We need to post the bike officers we have and some units from the inside at all of the garage entrances. Nobody goes in or out per Metro."

"What?" Matt said looking at me surprised, "What do you mean nobody goes in or out? How will people park?"

Stan came out from the back, "Post the officers, Matt. It's a crime scene until Metro clears it. Pull people out of the hotel if you have to, and put an officer at the walkway from the casino."

Matt posted the bike officers and a couple of guys from the casino at entrances and exits to the parking garage. A few more Metro Police cruisers arrived and they began to search the garage for any sign of a bullet. Matt posted Walter at the walkway from the casino to the garage and shortly, we could see people on camera walking through where Walter was supposed to stop them.

"Control to 278." Matt called over the radio.

"278 to Control go ahead." Walter came across.

"It looks like people are walking across the walkway to the garage! You're supposed to stop people from entering the garage from the casino!" Matt growled.

"Yeah, they're locals and they're going home. They just need to get to their car." Walter explained.

"The parking garage is a crime scene and we can't let anybody enter until it's been cleared by Metro!" Matt said.

"Yeah, but they want to go to their car." Walter said again.

"It's like some kind of magic dumb, isn't it?" I said smiling, "You'd swear this was just an act if you didn't know any better, wouldn't you?" I began to laugh.

"Control to Bike Three." Matt called.

"Bike Three, go ahead." Paul answered.

"Bike 3, intercept those people coming across the walkway and let them know they can't enter the garage." Matt said.

"They just need to get to their car!" Walter said sounding aggravated.

"Copy, and would you like me to put up a scarecrow or something at the entrance to keep other people from coming into the garage?" Paul answered.

I started giggling as the phone rang. "Security, this is Robert."

"Yes Robert, this is Nancy at the front desk. I'm getting complaints from employees and guests that security won't let them into the garage."

"That's correct, Nancy." I said nicely, "The garage is now a crime scene. Someone fired a weapon at one of our officers and now Metro is out there investigating."

"Well, I'm going to need you to let the front desk employees into the garage to get their cars." Nancy said.

"The garage is now a crime scene per Metro." I replied, "No one can enter it until it's been cleared by the police."

"Yes, but my people need to go home and the guests need to get to their cars!" Nancy sounded aggravated, "How long is this going to take?"

"You'd have to ask Metro," I answered, "It's their investigation."

Nancy hung up the phone. I made a mental note of how she acted for the next time I had to deal with her on the phone. I never liked people who would call up and demand things from me.

Roughly an hour and a half of not finding anything, Metro decided to clear the garage and open it back up. Matt sent our people back to their posts and the phone began to ring again. "Security, this is Robert."

"Hello Rober," a thickly accented voice said, "Dis is Juan in de Stewart's office. One of my employees was robbed."

"Your employee was robbed." I repeated a bit tired, "Where was he robbed?"

"In de garage, a black man take his wallet and money. He take twenty-two dollar!"

I looked over at Matt, "How long ago did this happen?"

"He say about two hour ago." came the reply.

"Two hours ago." I said now aggravated, "He was robbed two hours ago, but didn't bother to report it until now?"

"He wants to change into work clothes and clock in," I couldn't believe I was hearing this, "He tells me he want to report this on his first break."

"And how would he expect us to catch someone with a two hour head start?" I asked, "The guy could have gambled away the twenty-two dollars, had a drink, went into the club, picked up a girl and then left and still have time left to get away."

"The black man gamble the money?" asked the Stewart, "How you let him gamble the money?"

"How would I know if the black man....the suspect gambled the money?" I almost screamed, "You didn't bother to call about this for two hours!"

"You send someone for dis?" the Stewart asked.

"Yes, I'll send a supervisor, as a matter of fact!" I said sternly and hung up the phone.

I told Matt to send Stan down to the Stewart's office as the supposed robbery victim was someone down there. Just as Matt was calling Stan, someone began to beat on the dispatch door. I could hear someone yelling, too. I got up and looked through the peep hole in the door and saw Henry outside with two other cooks. Lovely.

I opened the door and Henry beamed at me. "Allo' Robair!" He said happily as he and the two cooks pushed three covered carts into dispatch. "Wa-la! I bring you lunch!" He shouted as he and his two assistants pulled the cover off of the carts.

Both Matt and I stared wide eyed at thick, prime rib steaks, lobster claws, mashed potatoes and gravy, and two large salads.

"You two do very good job!" Henry announced, "You deserve ze fabulous lunch! I 'ave ze best meat brought to me and do my own private recipe on zem! You 'ave French mashed and fluffed potato, fresh green salad and lobster claw! And for desert:" He whipped a cover off of a plate near the back of one of the carts, "French whipped Chocolate Moose!"

I didn't know what to say. I was used to not having any lunch out in dispatch and after the fiasco with Jack and the Police I hadn't thought I would get to even find a snack anywhere. I croaked out a quiet, "Thanks, Onrey."

He leaned over close and whispered to me, "You and only you may call me Henry. My American name for you, Ok?"

I smiled, "Ok, Henry. Thanks." The phone began to ring, and Henry began to scream at his assistants as they walked out of dispatch. "You call for ze dishes when you finish, oui?" He called as he left.

I smiled at all the food and answered the phone, "Security, this is Robert."

"Hi Robert, this is Stan. Still a bit busy out there?" Stan asked.

"Uh, sort of." I answered, "What's up?"

"I'm down here in the steward's office with the alleged robbery victim. They're telling me the guy who robbed him was in the casino gambling the money he took from the victim?"

"How do they know that?" I asked, "And who are *they*?"

"The supervisor here said you told him that." Stan explained.

"Ah, I see," I said, "Actually, I told him the guy could have been in the casino or anywhere since they waited two hours to report this."

"Miscommunication?" Stan asked.

"Well obviously he didn't get what I meant." I said a bit terse.

"I'll be adding his voluntary to the garage shooting report and then calling the Detective to have it picked up later." Stan said, "They're going to call you when his voluntary is completed, Ok? Have it picked up and brought to my office."

"You got it." I said, and hung up.

Dispatch had been pretty busy up to this point. I had dealt with busy nights before, but not with people coming and going in dispatch. So far a Police officer, Henry, Stan and the police Detective, and Paul had come and gone from dispatch. Things were turning into quite the madhouse!

Even as I was thinking I might have a minute's peace and time to eat my steak, the phone began to ring again. "Security, this is Robert."

"Yes, this is housekeeping. There's a naked man chasing a woman through the hallway." Came a female voice.

"Through the hallway," I repeated a bit distantly, "And what hallway is the naked man chasing the female *through*?"

"I don't know." Said the female, "Just a minute and I'll ask." I could hear her trying to call someone named "Maria" on her radio. After a few tries she came back on the phone: "I can't reach the person who called it in, just be on the lookout, ok?"

"Yeah." I said and hung up the phone. I turned to Matt, "There's a naked man chasing a female through the hallway."

"Which hallway?" He asked.

"Housekeeping doesn't know," I said, "They can't get some chick named *Maria* to answer the radio and actually give a location." I began to laugh as the phone rang again.

"Security, this is Robert."

"Yes, this is room 16011." A timid male voice said, "I'd like to report a crime."

"I see 16011." I said with a smile, "Please go right ahead and report it!"

"Ah, this girl was in my room. She took my money and stuff." said the voice.

"Ok, would you like to give me your name?" I asked.

"Do I have to?" he asked.

"Not at all," I replied, "You can hang up and I'll forget you called."

"Ok my name is ah…..Smith." he answered.

I cupped my hand over the receiver and looked over at Matt with a big grin, "His name is ah, Smith. And some chick took his money and stuff! Relative, maybe?"

Matt chuckled and I went back to the call, "So Mr. Smith, did you know this girl who allegedly robbed you?"

"I ah.....I met her in a bar." Mr. Smith said.
"And what?" I asked, "She pointed a gun at you? Picked your pocket? Did she rob you in the bar?"

"No." He answered.

"Wait a minute, I know!" I shouted, "You met her in the bar, took her up to your room for some unspecified activity, and then she took your stuff, right?"

"Right!" said Mr. Smith, "She took it when my back was turned!"

"Yeah, those hookers can be really sneaky, can't they?" I asked.

"Yeah, I guess.....wait, who said she was a hooker?" he said sounding almost panicked.

"It's called a *Trick Roll.*" I explained, "If you give me a description I can put it out to my officers and we can try to find her for you. Would you like me to send an officer up for a report?"

"NO!" Screamed Mr. Smith, "I'm here to get married! I can't let my fiancé find out about this! No reports! Can't you just give me back my money?"

"First of all, I didn't take your money so I can't give it back." I said indignantly, "And second of all, if you didn't want your fiancé to find out about a hooker, why would you pick one up and take her to your room?"

"Last fling!" He screamed, as if that would explain everything.

"Well, I'll ask again, would you like me to fling an officer up to your room for a report? Or maybe give me a description so I can try and find her?"

Mr. Smith hung up. I turned to Matt in mock surprise, "He hung up on me! He was trick rolled for a fling and then he hung up!"

"Are we sending anybody up?" Matt asked.

"Why?" I said, "He said he didn't want his fiancé to know he had a hooker up there and kept screaming *no reports*."

"I'd better ask Stan." Matt said.

"Don't ask Stan!" I whined, "He'll want a report for this and we don't even have any information!"

"Still, I need to ask Stan." Matt said as he started to dial the phone.

I sat glaring at him as he chatted with Stan. I watched him nod a few times and knew what was coming. After a minute he hung up and turned to me, "Stan wants to do a quick report on this and wants you to fill out a voluntary."

I sat staring at Matt. "You're a dickhead." I said. I turned and started to eat my steak.

I was shocked to find a few minutes without the phone ringing. I sat eating my steak and thinking. After a few minutes of thought, I looked over at Matt, "Why do you suppose we're here?" I asked.

"Somebody's got to work dispatch." He replied.

"No, I mean how did we end up in security?" I asked again.

"We applied." Matt answered simply.

"You're a huge help." I said as Matt smiled at me. I looked up at one of the monitors and realized for the first time that Officer Broderick's car was gone. "Hey," I asked Matt, "Where is Cortez?"

"He's with that cop looking for the puppet." Matt answered.

"Well, the cop's car is gone." I said pointing at the monitor, "I wonder how long it's been gone. Maybe you should check on Cortez."

Matt leaned towards the radio, "Control to 501." No answer. Matt tried again, "Control to 501." Nothing. He tried a third time; "Control to *501!*"

"Wow," I said, "He must be in a deep sleep somewhere. And you know, now that I think about it, we never got the call for Tom's escort to the theater."

"Control to 501!" Matt screamed into the radio. Still there was no response. "Control to all units, be on the lookout for 501. If anybody comes in contact with him, tell him to turn his radio back on!"

I began to absentmindedly hum the Twilight Zone theme. I looked over at Matt and began to laugh as he continued to call Cortez on the radio with no answer. He handled the shot taken at Jack really well, but Cortez not answering was stressing him out.

Finally after a few minutes, Cortez answered, "Go for 501"

"Oh, good morning 501!" Matt growled, "What's your status?"

"I'm still helping Metro." Cortez replied.

"Helping them do what?" Matt asked.

"Uh.....stuff, talking to people, and looking for the thing." Cortez answered

sleepily.

Matt looked over at me with a scowl on his face, "Stuff and talking to people.

The Metro Officer's car is gone. So how about I ask you again, what's your

status?"

"Oh uh.....he uh.....he just left, I was about to call you." Cortez stammered.

"I see, so you're clear?" Matt asked, "Then you can check on a sleeper over in

front of the Ambrosia."

"A what?" I asked, "Who called and said there was a sleeper there?"

"He lies to me, I lie to him." Matt replied.

I was really surprised a few quiet minutes passed that allowed me to eat the

food Henry had brought me. I looked over at Matt's food and he had only eaten

the steak. "Eat the mashed potatoes and other stuff, or Henry will get mad!" I

said to him.

"I don't want to eat the other stuff, I'm full." Matt replied.

"If we send the dishes back with food left on them he'll get mad and not send

us food again!" I insisted, "At least scrape off what you don't want to eat into the

trash and cover it with a paper!"

"How'd you get him to bring us food anyway?" Matt asked.

"Does it matter?" I answered, "Ditch the food so he'll be happy and we can get more someday."

With an exasperated sigh Matt got up to scrape uneaten food into the trash and once again the phone began to ring, "Security, this is Robert."

"Hey, this is Ralph from Engineering," came a somewhat familiar voice, "We've got a downed boiler that needs to be repaired."

"Ok, downed boiler." I repeated, "And you're going to work on that right now, right?"

"Ah…..no," said Ralph, "I'll be putting in a work order for dayshift."

"It's down. You aren't going to fix it?" I asked.

"Well, it needs to be repaired." Ralph said again, "So I'm putting in a repair order for dayshift."

"Who repairs the boilers, Ralph?" I asked, "Do Engineers do that?"

"Yeah….." Ralph answered, "The dayshift Engineers will repair it."

"Are you not an Engineer, Ralph?" I asked, "Do you repair *anything*? Why does everything have to be put in for dayshift to fix?"

"It's a boiler." Ralph answered.

"Yes, the boiler is down." I said again, "Why aren't you fixing it?"

"I'm putting in the work order!" Ralph shouted.

"Look Ralph," I started, "Why even call here and tell me…." Ralph hung up on me.

"You stupid, fucking, idiot!" I screamed into the receiver.

"Let me guess," Matt said looking over from a freshly emptied plate, "That was Ralph."

"What the hell do they pay that moron for?" I screamed, "To put in work orders all night? Hell, I should get his pay and I can put in the work orders for dayshift while I dispatch!"

Matt began to chuckle. "What's broken this time?"

"I don't know," I said, "He called and said a boiler was down or something. Why call us and say it's down? What the hell do we care?"

"I guess nothing else gets boiled now?" Matt chuckled, "Should we call Stan and let him know?"

"If you wanna." I said flatly.

"I'm serious," said Matt, "We should call Stan and tell him the boiler is broken!"

"He said the boiler is *down*," I insisted, "Not broken. Besides, there is more than one boiler in a place this big. Besides, what is Stan going to do? It's not our department."

"He can call somebody!" Matt insisted, "I'm gonna call him!" Matt picked up his phone and began to dial.

I picked up the phone myself and called the Ambrosia. I told the pleasant sounding lady who answered about Henry bringing us the food and let her know the dishes were ready to be picked up. She told me someone would be right over.

As I hung up Matt had a sour look on his face.

"You were right," Matt scowled, "Stan said there isn't anything he can do about Engineering unless it's some kind of emergency. But what if I need that boiler?"

"What do you need that particular boiler for?" I asked.

"I don't know!" Matt shouted, "But I might need it! I need it fixed right now!"

"What you need right now is to sit down and shut up." I giggled.

Matt scowled over at me, "I still think I'll need the boiler sometime in the near future."

"501 to Control." Came Cortez's voice over the radio, "Sleeper up and moving."

I looked over at Matt and began laughing. "You see?" I said, "He plays the lie game just as good as you do!"

"Copy 501, up and moving." Matt said into the radio.

"Maybe you should send Cortez to fix your boiler?" I asked, "I'm sure he'll tell you it's repaired after a little while of hiding." I began to laugh.

"111 to Control." Came Jack over the radio, "I've got a prior here at the Cloud Nine."

I rolled up the lounge on one of the monitors in front of me to find Jack standing next to Theresa the hooker. He seemed to be holding what looked like an ID."

"Hey, that's the chick I walked out something like three times last night!" I said giggling and pointing to the monitor, "She's like 19 or something, underage. I'll bet Jack will want to take her to the C.S.O.!"

"What's this female's name?" Matt asked over the radio.

"First of Brunhilda, and last of Swenson common spelling." Jack answered.

I began to laugh hysterically. "Brunhilda?" I giggled looking over at Matt.

"Uh…..standby." Matt answered Jack. He looked over at me laughing, "So what do we do, go with the name he's giving us?"

I continued giggling, but leaned over towards the radio, "111, show *Brunhilda* to the door, she's positive for a prior."

"What if that's her real ID?" Matt asked.

"Maybe she'll pull out a gun and shoot at him?" I asked jokingly. I looked over at Matt, "Haven't you walked this chick out a hundred damned times?"

"Well yeah, it *looks* like her…." Matt said.

"Weren't you a bouncer for crying out loud?!?" I asked hysterically, "You should know how easy it is to get a fake ID."

"Brunhilda." Matt said to himself.

"Something to name your first born!" I suggested and continued to laugh.

We watched on camera as Jack began to argue with the girl. Pretty soon she was waving her arms in the air and seemed to be screaming at him. He appeared to be screaming back and before long, they were nose to nose.

"Maybe you'd better send him some help?" I said to Matt.

"I think you're right." Matt said as he reached for the radio, "Control to 501."

I began to chuckle as I waited for Cortez to answer. But he didn't answer the first call.

"Control to 501." Matt tried again.

Now the girl pushed Jack. Jack grabbed her and threw her to the ground and began wrestling around with her.

"Better try someone else." I said.

"Control to available units, we have a fight near the Cloud Nine Lounge!" Matt screamed into the radio. Hank appeared on the monitor and began trying to sort out the wrestling match going on between Jack and the girl. He was doing pretty well until the girl swung one foot around and kicked him in the face. She tried to kick him again and this time a very angry looking Hank grabbed her leg and started dragging her around the floor! He used the leverage he could from holding her leg and quickly whipped her on to her stomach. Jack quickly put her in handcuffs.

I looked over at Matt who looked a bit stressed out, "Kind of like watching the Keystone Cops, isn't it?"

"The *who*?" he said looking back.

"Never mind." I answered, "Is the shift over yet?"

"Almost." Matt said.

Hank and Jack dragged the kicking, screaming girl to the C.S.O. door. "Make it hot!" Hank screamed into his radio as they walked inside. I pushed the record button on the VCR sitting next to me and started recording.

"We need to check you for….." Jack started to say, but before he could finish the girl turned her head and spit in his face. He staggered backward and Hank turned her around and sat her down on the C.S.O. bench.

"Now you sit there like a good girl," Hank said while backing away from her, "And we'll treat you right as long as you behave!"

The C.S.O. was the only place in the entire hotel with microphones inside so both video and sound could be recorded. I turned up the volume a bit and was ready to enjoy the show. Jack wiped off his face and sat down at a small desk. He picked up the phone and soon my phone was ringing.

"Hi Jack!" I answered brightly, "How are things on the casino floor?"

"Do you have a supervisor on the way here?" he said angrily.

"Do I?" I asked, "No. Maybe you should call one. Do they know you took this female to the C.S.O.?"

"You need to get me a supervisor!" Jack said and hung up the phone.

I looked over at Matt and smiled, "He wasn't very friendly! I can see why the women don't much care for him!"

Matt laughed as I picked up the phone and dialed the supervisor's office. "Security Office, this is Albert." said a sleepy voice.

"Hi Albert!" I said brightly, "We have one female in the C.S.O. Jack wants a supervisor up there."

"A female in the C.S.O.?" Albert repeated, "Why is someone in there? You guys know you're supposed to have permission to take somebody in there!"

"Yeah, but she seemed so nice," I said giggling, "Jack just couldn't resist!"

"Jack?" Albert asked, "What'd she do? Why'd he take her in there?"

"She's quite a girl," I continued to giggle, "I think her name is Brunhilda or something like that. She seems to have lots of energy!" I looked up at the monitor and could hear her screaming profanity at both Jack and Hank. She stayed on the bench, though.

The phone began to ring again, "Oh, another call! I have to go Albert, but you have fun now!" I hung up on Albert and answered the other line, "Security, this is Robert."

"Hi Robert, this is Ariana over at the Ambrosia." Said a pleasant voice, "Chef Onre' wanted me to call and find out how you enjoyed what he sent over to you tonight."

There was a knock at the dispatch door. I asked Ariana to hold for a minute and got up to see who it was. It was a young guy from the kitchen for the dishes. I pointed him to the room service carts and went back to the phone as he hustled them out the door.

"Oh, we loved the food!" I said happily as I turned up the volume in the C.S.O.

I cranked it up as loud as it would go. I held the phone near the speaker as I

talked, "It was wonderful, please let Henry know how much we appreciated it!"

From Ariana's pause I could tell all the profanity was coming through the
phone fine: "You fucking bastard! I'm going to have someone suck all the blood

out of you and then wear you like a coat! I'm going to have all your teeth

knocked out and then make you work a corner downtown! You can't do this to

me! You aren't a fucking cop, you loser!"

"Uh…..Robert, is everything ok there?" Ariana asked.

"Yeah, everything's under control, hold on a minute." I held the phone out and

screamed, "Shut your mouth you filthy, wino, whore! I'm talking on the phone!"

I smiled over at Matt who just shook his head and smiled back. "Sorry Ariana,

just Security business going on as usual! Tell Henry thanks again for the food!"

"You sleazy, fucking pig! I'm suing you! You and everybody in this

shithole!" Brunhilda continued to scream.

"Uh…..Ok. You have a nice night now. Good bye." Ariana said nervously

and hung up. I turned the C.S.O. volume back down and looked over at Matt

again.

"What do you suppose she'll tell him was going on in here?" I smiled.

"Who was it?" Matt asked.

"Ariana, from Ambrosia. Asking about the food." I said.

"Oh, she's stuck up." Matt said looking back at the monitor, "Who cares what she thinks went on in here?"

"Wouldn't give you any play, huh?" I laughed.

"No," Matt answered, "She's just a bitch. She doesn't like me, so I ignore her."
"You don't like anybody." I said turning back to the monitor and watching the

C.S.O. Albert walked into the C.S.O., and the girl directed her profanity towards

him right away.

"Oh great, someone in a cheap, fucking suit! Now we'll get to the bottom of

things!" she screamed.

Albert walked over to the desk where Jack sat, ignoring the girl. "What's the

deal?" he asked.

"She…..she pushed me!" Jack almost screamed, "And then she spit in my

face!"

Albert turned to Brunhilda, "Did you push him and then spit in his face?"

Brunhilda then spat at Albert as an answer.

"Why isn't she in a spitsock?" Albert asked.

"She…..she pushed me and spit at me!" Jack said again, "And then we brought

her in here! We didn't have time yet for a sock!"

I began laughing and turned to Matt, "Right desk drawer in the back?"

"Yup." Matt answered.

Albert began looking around the room. After looking in a cabinet he picked up

the phone and dialed dispatch: "Security, this is Robert." I answered.

"Uh yeah," Albert sounded confused, "Where are the….."

"Right desk drawer in the back." I said without letting him finish.

"Ah, yeah ok." Albert said and hung up. He opened the drawer and reached into the back pulling out a small plastic bag.

"Watch him put the plastic bag over her head and not the sock." I said to Matt joking.

Albert opened the bag and pulled out a white, mesh bag with a draw string. He quickly walked over and placed the bag over Brunhilda's head and then tightened the draw string just tight enough so she wouldn't be able to shake off the bag.

"There!" he announced, "Now you can spit all you want!"

I turned down the C.S.O. sound again after getting bored. Albert was calling the police and Brunhilda had quieted down a bit.

"So what do you think they found out about Mr. Funnybuns?" I asked Matt

Matt shrugged, "Who cares? I'd be shocked if they found out anything."

"Yeah….." I said thoughtfully.

The phone started to ring, "Security, this is Robert."

"Hi…..uh, why did they transfer me to you?" asked a male voice, "Do you guys handle this kind of stuff?"

"What kind of stuff?" I asked. I looked down at the caller ID and noted the hotel room that was calling me.

"We were looking for some girls to be sent up to the room. Are you the guys that do that?" He asked.

"No," I answered, "I don't send women anywhere."

"So.....can you transfer me to whoever handles the hookers then?" the man asked tentatively.

"Well," I said a bit sarcastically, "The police handle the hookers here in Vegas. You understand it's a crime here, right?"

"No it isn't," the male said, "Everybody knows you can get hookers when you come to Vegas!"

"Not only that," I replied in an absurdly over happy voice, "You can also get HIV, the clap, gonorrhea, herpes, and many other S.T.D's! Prostitution is illegal in Las Vegas. Most of the hookers here would probably rob you anyway. They aren't very nice. Grab the phone book in your room and look up the Chicken Ranch in Pahrump. It's legal there, and much safer."

"You.....you're lying about it being illegal, aren't you?" he asked.

"No, I'm not lying." I answered.

"Are you going to.....uh.....arrest us for this?" he asked sounding very nervous.

I sighed heavily, "First off, I'm not a cop, ok? I'm just hotel security. Secondly, why would I arrest you when you haven't done anything? All you did was call me and ask where the women are, right?"

"Yeah, I just asked about women!" he said sounding brighter.

"So call the Chicken Ranch, they'll probably be happy to send a car for you. And have a nice night, Sir." I hung up the phone.

I turned towards Matt: "Life pretty much seems to be in chaos when I'm telling some moron where to get a legal hooker. Are we almost done here?"

Matt glanced at the clock, "One more hour."

"Sheesh!" I moaned, "This night just went on and on! Damn it, I'm ready for my days off already!"

The phone began to ring again. I sat there and just looked at it. It rang a few more times and finally Matt picked it up, "Security, this is Matt."

I listened to him grunt a few times and then he asked the person on the phone, "Why would I care about that? Yes, I understand what you just said, why would I care? Yeah, same to you!" and then he hung up.

I looked over at Matt but he didn't say anything. After a minute I couldn't resist and finally asked, "What didn't you care about?"

He looked over at me confused. "You just asked somebody on the phone why you would care, what was that about?" I asked.

"Oh, some idiot from the pit telling me about a fill they were ordering," He said, "I think they thought I was surveillance."

"The dishes are gone, the police are gone, and Cortez is probably snoozing somewhere." I said looking at Matt, "Do you think things have finally calmed down?"

"Don't say that!" he screamed, "You're gonna jinx it! You say it's calm and then all hell's going to break loose!"

"All hell is not going to break loose!" I said looking back at the monitors, "Quit being superstitious!" I turned the volume up for the C.S.O. and noticed Albert had taken the spit sack off Brunhilda's head. He was standing in front of her reading her the trespass statement. She had calmed down, but didn't look too unhappy. Albert finished reading the statement to her. He handed her a clipboard with the trespass form on it so she could sign it. She signed and handed it back to him. I wondered when they had taken off her handcuffs, probably when the spitsock had come off.

"Ok, walk her out." Albert said to Hank and Jack.

A very sour looking Jack opened the door and followed Brunhilda out of the C.S.O. Hank trailed along behind. I could see Albert reaching for the phone and I grabbed my phone before the first ring had ended, "What's the deal? We just re-trespassed her and walked her out?" I asked.

"Metro's busy tonight," Albert said calmly, "They said it would be a few hours before they could respond."

"And Jack didn't want to sit there for a few hours waiting for a cop, huh? I asked.

"Oh yeah, he did," Albert said, "But I wasn't going to wait around that long, though. That's stupid to wait hours for them to maybe give her a ticket. She didn't have any warrants so they advised me it would be easier to just trespass her and let her go."

I looked over at Matt, "Albert's taking advice from Metro now." Matt giggled.

"Hey Albert, we were really busy out here tonight," I said, "How about you give us a no lunch and pay us an hour extra?"

Matt looked over at me, "I thought you said Stan would find out about the food?"

"Ah, who cares?" I said covering the phone.

"Oh yeah!" Albert said, "You guys did a great job out there tonight, I think Stan will ok a no lunch. I'll let him know. He should be in a good mood, tonight's his Friday."

"Yeah, I know." I said, "I wish it was my Friday! Are you doing the report on this trespass or would you like me to give it to Jack?"

"Oh, I'll do it." Albert said nicely, "I think Jack's still a bit upset I had him walk her out."

I began to laugh and hung up the phone. I quickly input a trespass report and turned to Matt, "No lunch!" I screamed, "I never got time to eat all that steak and lobster! Ha ha!"

The phone began its musical ring, "Security, this is Robert."

"Hi Robert, this is Metro Dispatch. How are you tonight?" Came a pleasant female voice.

"Uh, Well I *was* ok," I said, "I'm hoping you won't be changing that. How can I help you tonight?"

"We've had a 911 hang up at your hotel." She gave me the phone number and I recognized it as one near the showroom. A quick snicker escaped me as I thought about Mr. Funnybuns using a pay phone to try and call someone saying he had escaped from his abductors. I assured the dispatcher we would have an officer check it out and call them back if the police were needed. She thanked me and hung up.

I told Matt and had him dispatch someone to check on the phone. Matt dispatched Walter, and just as he finished, I pointed a camera towards the bank of pay phones where the call had come from.

"Look!" I screamed, "I think I see a small puppet running away from the phone!"

Matt leaned closer to the monitor, "What? Where?" he asked.

"Right there, right there!" I yelled, "I think Mr. Funnybuns escaped from whoever was holding him captive!" I burst out in loud laughter.

Matt just began shaking his head, "You're really weird." He said.

After a few minutes Walter called in and said the phone was code 4, which meant ok. We had been watching the phone bank with the camera I had put up, but Walter had never even walked near it.

"Where do you suppose he is?" I asked Matt.

"I don't know, smoking probably." Matt said sounding mad, "Control to 278."

No answer. Matt tried again, "Control to 278!"
Still nothing. I was tired, but Matt seemed both tired and frustrated.

"Control to 278!" He screamed into the radio again.

"278, go ahead." Walter finally answered.

"What's your location?" Matt asked, "Because we have the pay phone up on camera, but haven't seen you check it yet."

"Oh…..uh…..I checked it, you probably didn't see me." Walter replied.

I looked at my watch and saw a half an hour left in the shift. It reminded me of my last period in high school when I used to watch the clock.

"That's not what I asked you." Matt said, "What's your location?"

"I'm in the casino." Walter replied. As there was no background noise when Walter talked into his radio he probably wasn't in the casino.

"Ok, step back over to the phone so I can see you." Matt said.

The phone began to ring. "Security, this is Robert." I answered. I could hear myself sounding tired now.

"Hey Robert, tell your partner to let it go, ok?" came Stan's voice.

"Let it go?" I repeated it as a question.

"Yes, let it go." Stan said again, "If you guys can see the phone on camera and things look ok, let it go."

"You're the boss." I said and hung up. I turned to Matt, "Stan says to let it go, everything's ok because we can see the phone on camera."

"What?" Matt said sounding outraged, "What if someone's hurt that we can't see? I'm not going to let it go! Walter needs to do his damned job!" He picked up the phone and dialed Stan's office.

I listened to him argue with Stan for a while over someone he couldn't see and then began tuning him out. On the monitor after a few minutes Walter appeared in front of the pay phone and started waving. He didn't seem to have any idea where the camera was and so was waving in all directions. I chuckled to myself at how funny he looked.

Matt hung up the phone hard and then almost screamed, "That is *bullshit*!"

"Let it go, it's almost the end of the shift." I said.

"He needs to do his job and not hide!" Matt growled at me.

"Who cares?" I asked, "It's not like complaining to Stan today is going to change anything. Walter will still be useless tomorrow. He pulls this same shit every night and you know it!"

"I know." Matt said, "But it just isn't right!"

I looked at my slowly ticking watch. 25 minutes left. Sheesh, time was dragging. Matt was tired and frustrated, I was tired and frustrated; it was time to go home. I couldn't wait to be relieved. We sat in silence for the next 20 minutes.

Just before we were relieved I noticed a man wearing what looked like a sheet standing outside near the main entrance. I zoomed the camera in on him and saw he was holding a sign and screaming at people as they walked by. As I was watching him, the phone began to ring. It was the bell desk telling me about the man in the sheet harassing people as they walked into the hotel.

Our relief finally walked in the door as I was watching the man.

"So," one of the relief officers named John said, "You guys had a shooting tonight, huh?"

"Look at this." I said ignoring his question. I zoomed in closer on the man in the sheet. "I don't think he has anything on under the sheet!" I began to laugh.

"Is that a sign he's carrying?" John asked, "What's it say?"

"I don't know." I answered as I got up so he could take my chair near the phone, "He won't hold it still enough for me to read it." As I said that, the man began swinging the sign at a bellman trying to talk to him.

"Have you guys sent anybody out there yet?" John's partner an officer named Mike asked.

"Nope." Matt said, "He just showed up, he's all yours."

"Nothing else to pass on, except for the man in the sheet." I said as Matt and I made for the door. I could hear Mike calling his units to respond to the main entrance for the man.

"What a night, huh?" I said to Matt as we walked down the hall, "Puppets and guns, hookers and shit? Quite a night!"

Matt just grunted back at me. He was moving at a quick step towards the briefing room to clock out and go home. I gave up talking to him and saw Paul as we got into the briefing room.

"Pauly!" I called as I walked up to Paul, "Wasn't tonight fun?"

"Oh yeah," He replied, "It was a blast. I love keeping people out of the garage."

Matt hustled Stan out of his office so he could adjust the time clock for us and give us the extra hour for not getting lunch. Paul stood waiting for us to clock out so he could walk out with us.

"So, did they ever find out anything about that puppet?" Paul asked me.

"How would I know that?" I answered, "Do they tell me anything? Do I know the outcome of anything at all?"

Paul smiled as I rambled, "So nobody knows where the puppet is, huh?" He said winking at me.

"Stop winking at me." I said, "I don't know anything. And if I did, I still wouldn't know anything! Why don't you ask me where the bullet is that they didn't find?"

"Ok." Paul said, "Where's the bullet they didn't find?"

I sighed and just shook my head. Stan adjusted our hours and we started walking out towards our cars.

"So where was Walter?" Paul asked Matt as we walked.

"He doesn't do his job!" Matt began screaming again.

"He doesn't?" Paul asked winking at me again, "What do you mean? What job doesn't he do?"

Matt turned and glared at Paul.

"I love to spin him all up!" Paul said to me laughing!

"You love to spin everybody all up." I replied, "I think it's time to hit the sack and sleep until the next shift."

"Time for beer and tequila you mean?" Paul asked. Matt nodded at this.

"I think not." I said, "Maybe something to eat and then it's off to dreamland. Hopefully it will be more peaceful there than it is here at Paradise.

We got out to our cars and I opened my door. "Do we really like what we do?" I asked Paul before I got in my car. "Is this really what we wanted to be when we grew up?"

"It pays the bills." Paul replied, "Besides, what else could be this funny and this much fun?"

"I guess you're right." I said as got into my car. I wondered what would happen tonight while I was on the radio in dispatch. I started my car and drove out of the parking garage.

Chapter Five
Radio Chaos

Returning to work, I looked forward to getting through my shift and leaving. This was the last workday of the week for me, my Friday as we called it. It was my turn to run the shift by working the radio side of dispatch. Matt would be out there with me again working the phone side. He would ask me to take the phones and let him work the radio side like he always did, but I would tell him no like I always did.

The Strip was busy as I drove into work so I knew the Golden Paradise would be packed. More people, more trouble. Part of me hoped it would be a really busy night. Busy nights always seemed to go by quickly. I was ready for my days off and would be really happy to have the shift go by quickly. I walked into the briefing room and took my usual seat. Paul and Matt weren't there yet, so I just sat quietly and waited for briefing to start.

Paul and Matt eventually strolled in together about five minutes before briefing. They both greeted me and sat down.

"Let's hope things stay quiet tonight." Matt said as he attempted to put on his gear. "How about I take the radio side tonight and maybe things will stay calm like last night."

"Calm as in Jack getting shot at, the police coming about a missing puppet, and people going to the C.S.O?" I asked.

"Well, things definitely could have been worse." Matt shrugged.

"Is that so?" I turned and looked at him, "And how could it have been worse?"

"Well…. ah…. they could have hit Jack when they shot at him." He said quietly.

"Oh yeah, that would have been just horrible." I growled, "And who the hell are *they*? Nope, radio's mine tonight."

I turned to Paul, "And how are things in the retired military world?"

Paul looked up at me, "What?"

"What? Are you deaf?" I asked.

"Huh?" Paul repeated, "Speak up; you're talking into my deaf ear."

"I thought I was talking to your face, not into an ear." I said quietly while turning away.

"Well, speak louder to the face next time." Paul said with a smile.

Walt came out to the podium for the night's briefing and began shuffling some papers.

"Do you think he'll say anything important tonight?" I asked to no one specific.

"Who, him?" Paul pointing towards Walt, "I don't think anybody ever says anything important here." I chuckled to myself.

Walt looked around the room and tried shuffling the papers again. The room didn't get any quieter; people were still milling around and chatting away with each other.

Finally, Walt tried verbally, "Can I have some attention up here, people? This is my time, now!"

I glanced over at Matt; "It's his time now, shut up."

"I wasn't saying anything!" Matt whined.

"Come on, people!" Walt kept trying, "You need to stop talking and let me have my time now!" The room quieted down a bit. "It's really busy up in the casino and I have a lot of things to go over, ok?"

"A busy casino," I mumbled to myself, "Imagine that?"

Walt continued on: "First off, we have a new memo that says the casino hosts will now be able to comp golf games to certain players. They will be able to comp no more than eighteen holes a day, though."

"Miniature golf?" I piped up.

"Are we casino hosts?" Paul asked over me, "Can we now comp things?"

Walt ignored me and answered Paul, "Were you a casino host before? Does the patch on your sleeve say host? What makes you think you would be a casino host now?"

"You're reading a memo to us about what casino hosts can comp. Why read it to us if we aren't hosts?" Paul said.

"Maybe you'll have someone ask about golf while you're working. You can tell them hosts can comp them some games!" Walt said nastily.
"No more than eighteen holes a day of miniature golf, though!" I spouted.

"Who is going to ask me about comps outside? The employees in the parking lot? The guests in the garage?" Paul asked, "I'm a bike unit. Usually all I get asked is where someone can park. They usually ask it while sitting in front of a parking place!"

"Can the hosts comp golf clubs, too?" I asked, "How about carts, or a caddie?

"What about *balls*?" Paul asked giggling.

"*Stop this*!" Walt screamed at us, "Let me read the memo! If you have questions, please feel free to call a host and ask! All I'm here for right now is to read all these memos! Now I have a lot to go over tonight, so stop all this stupidity!"

"If the memo was written *to* the hosts, how could they answer questions about it?" I asked, "Who wrote the memo? Maybe I should ask them? Was this memo even sent to them?" Walt wadded up the memo and threw it at me. He missed by a good distance and I smiled back at him.

"Next, there was an incident in the Ambrosia last night and they want us to do half hour checks of the restaurant. Just walk through and show our presence, ok? Let me know immediately if there is any kind of problem."

"Uh, what kind of incident prompted this?" Matt asked.

"Someone didn't get their golf comp." I said with a smile. Several other officers started to laugh.

"I guess things got a bit out of control with some guests. There was some kind of altercation." Walt answered.

"It was a big food fight." someone in the back said.

"Yes," Walt said, "There was a big food fight in the restaurant. We received many complaints about the time it took for security to arrive and stop it."

"Is that so?" I said giggling and looking at Matt.

"Yes, that's so!" Walt said glaring at me, "So we need to do a walk through every half hour or so, ok"

"Got it," I said, "Please continue."

"We're still missing the puppet from the Jester's Court." Walt continued, "Everyone needs to be on the lookout for this puppet, Metro has already been here and did a report on it."

"*We* are?" Paul giggled, "I thought it was Tom Triphorn's."

Matt turned and looked over at me. But I kept looking forward at Walt.

"Mr. Sam Silverton was promoted to full engineer this week and the executives would like all of us to congratulate him when we see him." Walt continued.

"What was he before?" I asked.

"A partial engineer." Paul said, and I started to laugh.

"We just need to congratulate him when we see him." Walt said with a smile.

"I don't even know who he is," I retorted, "How am I supposed to know him when I see him?"

"Just congratulate everyone with a nametag that says *Sam* on it." Matt mumbled.

"Then don't congratulate him," Walt said, "I don't care either way. Moving on…"

"Horrible attitude!" I said shaking my head, "Simply horrible!"

"Maybe we need to comp Walt a golf game?" Paul asked.

"Maybe," I said, "But not more than eighteen holes, and no clubs or colored balls."

"Colored balls?" Paul asked, "Walt has colored balls?"

"*Moving on!*" Walt screamed over us, "For those of you who weren't here last night, we had a robbery suspect take a shot at an officer out in the garage. We need to stay vigilant and keep dispatch informed about anything suspicious, ok? Everyone did a great job last night, but we need to stay on our toes and be careful out there."

"Maybe we shouldn't chase people with guns?" I whispered to Matt.

"We have a large crowd at the 8 Star club tonight," Walt continued, "So we need to take walks by the entrance to the club and make sure there are no problems with the line."

"Uh, isn't that the responsibility of the club bouncers to watch the line?" Matt asked.

"While it's in our casino, it's our responsibility." Walt answered, "We don't need problems spilling out away from the club."

"Bike 3, do you have anything new for us about firearms practice?" Walt asked Paul.

"Anything new?" Paul asked in return, "I don't have anything old for you about that."

"Weren't you supposed to get with the training director and find out about practice?" Walt asked.

"No, I think the training director should get with *you* about practice." Paul retorted, "Management should be handling something like this, don't you think? You can't just schedule something without talking to me and then expect me to just come in for it. I do have a life, you know!"

I turned towards Paul and said, "Nothing but Paradise matters."

"Is Paradise raising my kids?" Paul asked.

"Maybe." I said with a smile.

"They're sending me memos that say you'll be handling firearms practice." Walt said looking down at a paper in front of him.

"Who are *they*?" I turned around and asked Paul with a smile.

"I'll send you a memo later that says I'm not, Ok Walt?" Paul said

"I'll have to get with you later about this." Walt said wrinkling his brow, "Are there any more questions about anything I've went over tonight?"

"How many holes of golf are we allowed to comp?" I asked smiling.
Walt ignored me, "Then let's have a safe night. I'll be in my office working on the schedule if anyone needs me."

Walt went back into his office and everyone got up and started to leave the briefing room. I stood up and looked at Paul, "So, when is firearms practice?"

"Go comp your golf." He laughed and headed towards the door.

Matt and I went into Walt's office to pick up the night's roster. "So the 8 Star is pretty busy tonight, huh? What's going on inside there to make tonight so special?"

"Do I know?" Walt asked, "I get told just as much as you do, probably less! Maybe there's some celebrity inside or something, I don't know."

"A celebrity?" I asked looking at Matt, "I wonder who it is? I'll have to call one of the bouncers and ask who's in there."

"Don't be harassing the bouncers!" Walt said looking at me now, "I don't need to deal with any complaints from any of the people in that club tonight! You behave yourself, understand?"

"I'm appalled you'd say that to me!" I said getting all huffy, "I'm always good! I never misbehave!"

I looked over at Matt with an evil grin. "What?" Matt said defensively, "Don't look at me; I'm always good, too!"

I picked up the roster sheet. Matt and I sauntered off towards dispatch. "Bye Walt!" I screamed as we walked out the door.

We walked down the hall not saying a word. Finally, I broke the silence, "I'm so glad this is my Friday!"

"Not for me, not this week." Matt said.

"No?" I asked, "You're off the same days I am. How is this not your Friday?"

"Ok, it's my Friday," Matt answered, "But I have overtime the next two nights. So I'll just keep on working until next week."

"You're kidding me, right?" I asked, "You took overtime for *both of your days off*? Are you nuts? You need some time away from this stuff; you're going to get all stressed out with no days off!"

"I'll take some days off when I need them." Matt said, "For now, I need the extra money."

"It's your life and your time." I said as we got to the dispatch door, "Feel free to stress yourself out as much as you'd like.

We opened the dispatch door and found complete chaos. Phone lines were ringing, both dispatchers from the other shift were on lines and they looked really worn out. Dispatch would do that to you.

The guy on the radio hung up the phone and then turned quickly to me before answering the next line, "We've got a medical in room 40123, and some guy split his head open and we're rolling the paramedics." He picked up the phone,

"Security, Roger."

I looked at Matt, "Lovely, starting out with a medical already."
Matt smiled, "I can still take the radio if you want."

"I don't think so." I smiled, "I'm quite certain I can handle a guy with his head

split open."

"Do you guys have someone to send to the medical?" Roger asked.

"Yeah," I answered, "Send Phil, 191"

Roger dispatched Phil to the room. I sat down in another chair waiting until he

was ready to give up his spot in front of the radio. The phones seemed to have

calmed down for the moment. I watched as Roger and his partner gathered their

paperwork and personal items. "I've had it! It's all yours!" Roger said and got

up.

I chuckled a bit as I sat down. All the dispatchers always seemed to be

exhausted at the end of a busy shift. Trying to control a shift of Paradise security

officers always seemed to make us more tired than walking around the casino. I

readied myself to deal with the accident when the paramedics arrived. I set the

monitors on the cameras I wanted to watch. Matt eventually sat down beside me

and we dove right into the chaos.

The phone rang and Matt answered it. A minute later he told me it was for me.

"Security, this is Robert."

"Hi Robert, it's Phil." came Phil's voice.

"Hi Phil, the paramedics should be on the way. What happened up there?"

"Well, this guy's pretty uncooperative. There's blood all over the place and now he's saying he's missing some money." Phil said

"Trick roll?" I asked, "Robbed by one of those stupid hookers?"

"Ahhh, not according to him." Phil said, "He says he fell out of bed and split his head on the nightstand. Funny thing is there really isn't any blood on the nightstand. Then he starts telling me he's missing five hundred dollars."

"Missing five hundred, huh?" I said, "But he says the two incidents aren't related, right?"

"Exactly," Phil said, "He bumped his head on the night stand and now the money's gone. But he says no one was up here with him."

"I see." I said, "Ok, we'll have to do two separate reports on this. A guest accident for the cut head, and a missing property for the money. Will he be able to fill out a voluntary about the missing money?"

Matt turned to me, "The paramedics are on property and Jack is taking them up to the room."

"He says he won't fill out a voluntary and keeps demanding I give him back his money." said Phil.

"Did you take his money?" I asked.

"Of course not!" Phil said, "I explained to him about doing the report and doing a lock interrogation to find out what keys were used to enter the room and then he got all hostile!"

"I see," I said, "Maybe the nightstand took his money? Would he like to press charges against the nightstand?"

"Now he wants a supervisor." Phil said, "He's demanding to know why we're trying to investigate him."

"Tell him we're investigating the nightstand." I said getting bored with the conversation, "And we think it's hiding something."

I could hear screaming over the phone as the man kept yelling at Phil. "He keeps demanding a supervisor," Phil said, "And I'm getting really tired of listening to him. Can you send me another officer?"

"Don't worry," I reassured Phil, "Jack's on the way with the paramedics and I'll send Walt or Albert up there for you."

Phil thanked me and hung up. I chuckled to myself and dialed the supervisor's office.

"Security Office, this is Walt." came Walt's voice.

"Hey Walt; it's Robert!" I said happily, "Guess what I've got for you?"

"We're in the middle of a medical call, right?" Walt said calmly, "I already know about that."

"But did you know the man claims a nightstand hit him and then took his money? He wants a supervisor to go up there and give him his money back. Can you please respond to room 40123."

"What?" Walt asked, "Someone hit him with a nightstand?"

"Ah...no," I said trying not to laugh, "He says the nightstand hit him and took his money. Someone didn't hit him *with* the nightstand; the nightstand itself hit and robbed him."

"You're making this up to bother me, aren't you?" Walt said suspiciously.

I began to laugh. "No, really Walt! Phil needs a supervisor up there. I guess the guy is claiming to have been robbed, but says he hit his head on the nightstand while he was sleeping. He really is demanding a supervisor, though."

"The paramedics are on scene in room 40123." Matt said looking over at me.

"Fine," Walt said, "I'm on my way up, what was the room number again?"

"40123." I repeated, "Hey, is Albert here yet?"

"Albert called and said he was going to be about an hour and a half late tonight." Walt answered.

"Did you tell him the bar won't close in an hour and a half," I chuckled, "They stay open all night here."

"Ha, ha." Walt said and hung up.

The phone rang. The caller ID said it was coming from room 40123. Matt picked up the phone, "Security, this is Matt. Really? Oh really? Is that so?" Matt looked over at me and smiled. He hung up the phone and said, "Guess what?"

"I'll bet the nightstand confessed and then tried to jump out the window, right?" I said with a big smile.

"You're close," Matt said, "I guess the guy got nasty with the paramedics and they determined he was a danger to himself. Now he's going bye, bye."

"No!" I said laughing again, "He was full of some goofballs or something?"

"Oh yeah, Phil says they are strapping him down to the gurney now. I could hear him screaming in the background."

I called Walt on the radio and asked him to call dispatch before he got to the room. Better to let him know what he was walking into. Walt called and Matt began to brief him on what was going on as another line began to ring.

"Security, this is Robert." I said nicely.

"Uh…yes, this is Mr. Stenson." came a voice. I looked at the caller ID and noticed it was coming from 40122, next door to where the paramedics were.

"Yes Mr. Stenson," I said nicely, "How can I help you tonight?"

"I think someone is being attacked next door!" Mr. Stenson said lowering his voice. I could hear someone screaming *No!, No!, No!* over the phone. "I think they're trying to drag a guy off!"

"I wouldn't worry about that, Sir." I said nicely, "We have the paramedics and some officers up in the room next to yours. They're taking care of whatever's going on in there. Everything will be fine, I'm very sorry you were disturbed by the noise."

"Are you sure?" Mr. Stenson asked, "Things sound like they're getting pretty violent over there."

"Oh, yes Sir." I said trying hard to still sound pleasant. "Everything is under control. I'm certain things will be resolved pretty quickly." I could hear another phone line ring and Matt answering it.

"Oh, Ok." Mr. Stenson said, "As long as you're sure things are under control."

"Oh yes, we know what we're doing. Everything's under control." I lied.

I hung up the phone and could hear Matt telling someone else the same thing I had told Mr. Stenson. I wondered if we would get complaints from every room on the floor. Not surprisingly, the phone rang again. This time it was the Front Desk.

"Security, this is Robert." I said, fairly sure what it would be about.

"Hi Robert, this is Nancy from the front desk." I recognized her as one of the managers.

"Hi Nancy," I said happily, "How's the night going for you so far? Are you having as much fun as I am?"

"No fun, no." Nancy answered, "We're getting calls from guests on the fortieth floor about someone being attacked up there in a room."

"Really?" I asked, "Someone being attacked on forty, huh? I don't know about anyone being attacked, but we have someone on a controlled substance being taken away by the paramedics in room 40123. Maybe he's unhappy about that?"

"Someone in that room is being *taken away*?" Nancy asked, "You mean he's being forcibly removed from the room?"
"Uh, actually it's probably more like he's being forcibly removed from society for both his and everyone else's safety. At least for now." I said.

"And Security is removing this person from society and the room?" Nancy asked.

"No, no," I explained, "The paramedics are up there with this guy. They determined he was on something that made him unsafe, I guess. They're taking him away. We just take them up to the room and help if they ask."

"I see," Nancy said, but I got the feeling she didn't understand, "So what is the person's name who's being removed, and what was he supposedly on?"

"Sorry, I don't have that info just yet," I said, "But I'm sure the officer doing the report on this will be down to talk to you shortly."

"Ah, Ok." Nancy said, "As long as everything's under control. Make sure he let's me know what's going on as soon as possible."
"No problem." I said and hung up the phone.

I looked over at Matt as he was hanging up the phone. "More noise complaints from forty?" I asked.

"Yeah." He answered, "What do you suppose is really going on up there?"

I waggled my fingers at Matt and said, "Hooooo! The Evil Nightstand is attacking people! Hooooo!" I began to laugh hysterically. Matt glared at me.

The phone rang again. Matt answered it. He put the person on hold and said it was for me. I picked up the phone wondering what chaos this would be: "Security, this is Robert."

"Hey, Bro! It's Sammy! How you been doin'?" came a familiar voice. It was one of the bouncers from the 8 Star club.

"Hey Dude!" I said, "I've been ok, what's up?"

"I was wondering, Bro if you could do me a solid?" he asked.

"618 to control." more radio traffic.

"Hold on a minute Sammy, I've got something going on." I said quickly, "Go ahead 618." I said into the radio. I looked over at Matt who just shrugged at me.

"618 to Control, there are some officers and paramedics tying a guy to a bed up here; should I help out?"

"Are you working overtime?" I asked. "Your shift ended 15 minutes ago. What are you still doing in the hotel?"

"They're tying him to one of those paramedic beds." 618 said, "Should I be helping them?"

"Once again 618," I said, starting to lose my patience, "Your shift *ended* 15 minutes ago. Why are you still in the hotel?"

"He keeps screaming!" came 618's reply, "I don't think he wants to go with the paramedics. But they're tying him down to the bed."

I told Sammy he would have to call me back in a little bit for his "solid" and turned to Matt, "Do you believe this?"

"Control to 618, why are you still in the hotel?" I asked a bit sternly.
"Ok, now they're wheeling him down the hall to the elevators." 618 said, "I'm going to follow them and see what happens."

"Control to 618." I called. No response, "Control to 618!" I tried again. Finally I gave up and leaned back in my chair. I looked over at Matt, "Tell me I don't really work with people this stupid."

"Oh; they're this dumb, alright!" Matt said with a smile.

"111 to Control!" Jack called over the radio.

"Go ahead, 111." I answered.

"It's going to be a positive transport to Spring Valley." Jack said correctly. I might enjoy teasing Jack and didn't really get along with him, but at least he knew how to call in some things in over the radio.

I wrote down the transport location on the log sheet in front of me. Matt adjusted one of the cameras so we could see the struggling male on the gurney as he was loaded into the back of the ambulance.

"618 to Control." I just ignored the annoying voice.

"618 to Control?" this time as a question. "618 to Control, if you can hear me, he's being put in an ambulance now. I think they're going to take him away."

I looked over at Matt with a big smile. "This has to be an act, right? Nobody's really this dumb!" Matt smiled back and shook his head.

"No act." Matt said, "I'm pretty sure he's really this dumb for real."

"Bike Three on two!" Paul said over the alternate channel, "Since they're taking the guy to the hospital on a bed, would the nightstand like to go, too? Or does it want to press charges?"

I began to laugh and pressed the alternate channel transmit button, "No, I think Walt is still upstairs trying to wrestle the nightstand into custody. We may need SWAT."

"618 to Control, I think my watch stopped." he persisted, I was so glad this person was not on my shift, "Can you tell me what time it is?"

"Time to get a new watch." I answered sarcastically.

The phone rang. Matt answered it. He said, "Yes, Sir" a few times and hung up.

"Walt says to not be sarcastic and send the guy downstairs to clock out." Matt said with a smile.

"Oh, *Walt said*!" I said huffily, "Then I'd better obey because *Walt said so*! Oh yeah, we'd better run for the hills because *Walt* said so!" I leaned in to the radio, "Control to 618." No answer, "Control to 618." Still no answer. I looked over at Matt. "Earth to 618, are you in deep space yet?" Still nothing, not even another mad call from Walt. I was disappointed, I guess I would have to try harder if I wanted to aggravate people, "Moonbase Alpha to 618; repeat,

Moonbase Alpha to 618, how's the weather out there in La, La Land?"

A minute later came that annoying voice, "618 to Control, did you have traffic for me? I've been watching the guy in the ambulance."
"Control to 618, please go downstairs." I said.

"You want me to go downstairs?" 618 answered, "Don't you need me to keep helping with the paramedics?"

"What are you helping them do?" I asked.

"Oh, I'm just here in case anything happens." 618 replied.

I looked over at Matt, "How do these people survive in life this long without dying?"

Matt chuckled and shook his head.

"618, you need to go downstairs now!!" I screamed.

"Ok, but if you need me give me a call." he answered.

"Do you think you'll be needing 618 for anything?" I asked Matt.

"I really doubt it." Matt said laughing.

"Maybe we could have him come out here if it's slow and throw darts at him, or something?" I asked. Matt continued to laugh.

The phones began to ring again. Matt picked up a line and so did I, "Security, this is Robert."

"Hey Bro, it's Sammy again. Are you still busy?" asked Sammy.

"I don't know," I said, "Is the club still busy?"

"Oh, we're packed!" Sammy said excitedly, "It's because of that guy who's here."

"Oh yeah!" I said, remembering Walt mentioning a celebrity was in the club, "We heard some celebrity was in there, who is it?"

"It's that guy from the thing." Sammy answered, "You know, the thing!"

"What thing?" I asked, "What guy? What nonsense is this? What's his name?"

"I don't know." Sammy said sounding really puzzled, "But you know him. He's the guy from the thing! You know, the thing!"

"Ok, I'm only going to tell you this once," I said, "Stop saying *The Thing*. Is he in movies, TV, or what?"

"Yeah, yeah!" Sammy said, "Exactly! You know, he's in the.... the stuff, he does that stuff."

"Ok," I stopped Sammy, "I've had enough of the Abbot and Costello shit. What's the *solid* thing you wanted?"

"The solid?" He sounded confused.

"Yes, the solid." I said starting to lose my patience, "You called me for a reason, what did you need?"

"Oh yeah, Bro!" he sounded excited again, "I met this hottie and she said she really wanted to go to the show! You know, the one with the guy!"

"The show with the guy." I said dully, "The guy from the thing."

"Yeah!" He seemed to think I knew exactly what he was talking about, "I guess she loves that guy! Can you get some tickets for me? From that chick you used to know?"

"Chick I used to…" I suddenly knew what he wanted, "Oh! You want to go to the Jester's Court and see Tom, right?"

"Yeah, Bro!" He sounded more hopped up than ever, "Yeah, Tom! The guy from the thing!"

"Uh, it really wasn't me who…" I started, "Well, I guess I do know her. I'll see what I can do, but she might want something in return. You know that, right?"

"In return?" Sammy's excitement seemed to melt away.

"She might want to take somebody in the club." I explained, "You know, kind of a trade off. You let some of her friends inside the 8 Star without paying the cover charge, and she gets you a couple of comps."

"Yeah, Bro!" the excitement returned, "I could do that, I can get her in! I could even get her a table and some drinks, I know the bartenders!"

"I would think you do, being one of the bouncers." I said, "Maybe you could even let her meet the guy from the thing?"

"Oh, he's in a V.I.P. room," Sammy said, not getting my sarcasm, "He doesn't really like people to come and meet him."

"Let me see what I can do and I call you back, ok?" I asked.

"No problem, Bro! Take care!" Sammy said and hung up.

Matt was finishing up with his second phone call. I looked over at him, but before I could talk, he started telling me I had two new calls to put out.

"You've got a missing property in room 6014 and a guest complaint in 8111. They are upset because someone rumpled their bed up while they were out of the room." Matt said.

"Someone rumpled their bed?" I asked, "You mean it was messed up? Like someone slept in it?"

"No." Matt answered, "I asked that, too. They said the bedspread looked like someone had laid on it or something. So they're all unhappy."

"You're kidding me? Maybe the nightstand was in there." I said, wrinkling my brow, "Never mind, don't answer that. Control to 111."

"111 go ahead." came Jack's response. He seemed to be on the ball a bit tonight.

"111, when you're clear head up to room 8111 for a missing property report." I said.

"Copy Control." Jack replied, "I'm clear now, I'll head right up."

"Control to 723."

Matt looked over at me, "You aren't going to send Hank on the guest complaint, are you?"

"Yeah, why not?" I asked.

"You know what he's like!" Matt said, "If it's something stupid, he'll get all upset!"

"So?" I replied, "Is it something stupid?"
"Go ahead Control." Hank replied.

"Pick up some paperwork and head up to 6014 for a guest complaint report. Give us a call when you get all your info, ok?"

"Copy, 6014." Hank said.

"Walt's gonna call you." Matt said. The phones didn't ring, though. "He's gonna call, I'm telling you! Hank gets all upset!"

"Oh be quiet!" I said, "I'll handle Walt. Hey, do you remember Wendy Shu?"

"You know I do." Matt said looking at me suspiciously, "Where is this going?"

"Uh…well maybe you could…uh, I don't know, give her a call for me?" I asked.

Matt scowled, "What do you think the answer to that is? You know she won't even talk to me anymore!"

"Well, I need a comp to see Tom's show." I said, "So I thought maybe you could…."

Matt cut me off, "Hey, what happened wasn't my fault! The other girl came on to *me*! What was I supposed to do? She was too jealous and possessive!"

I started to laugh, "I just wanted you to give her a call." Matt continued to bellow and scream as I picked up the phone and dialed the Jester's Court box office.

"Jester's Court Theater, laugh til' you ache." A pleasant voice answered.

"Hi, this is Robert from Security," I said, "Can I speak with Wendy, please?"
"Sure." She said, "Let me put you on hold while I get her."

I listened to a scratchy voice tell me about the wonderful places in the hotel. It informed me of how the Spa would relax you, how the nightlife was incredible in the 8 Star Club, and many other wonderful things. I thought to myself they should add, *"Come and see the guy from the Thing!"* to the recording.

"Hello, this is Wendy." Wendy said, "How can I help you tonight?"

"Hi Wendy, it's Robert from Security!" I said brightly, "Do you by chance remember me?"

"Of course!" Wendy said I could almost hear the smile through the phone, "How are you?"

"Oh, doing pretty good; surviving." I answered, "Listen, I was wondering if you could do me a big favor?"

"Sure," Wendy answered, "What do you need?"

"I've got a friend in the 8 Star who was asking me about a couple of comps for Tom's show." I explained, "Is there any way you can help me out?"

"No problem." she replied, "What day does he need them for?"

"You know, I don't really know. I never asked him." I answered, "I didn't know it would be this easy!" I began laughing.

"How's Matt?" she asked.

I looked over at Matt, who was now scowling at the monitors, "Oh, he's fine. Still gets a little exited at times, you know."

"Yes, I know all about Matthew." Wendy giggled.

"Hey, I told my friend you might want to get some people into the 8 Star sometime in exchange for this, so that's out there if you want it. He might even be able to get you a table and a few drinks!"

"That sounds great!" Wendy said, "Is that open for anytime?"

"I'm sure it is." I answered, "He's a pretty good guy. In fact, he's working the front door right now if you want to talk to him! Just go ask for Sammy. I can let him know you'll be looking for him, or I can send him to see you if you want."

"I will go see him." Wendy said, "I need to get out of the office anyway. I'd love to sit in the club and have a drink tonight! You said his name is Sammy?"

"Yeah," I answered, happy I could get a friend a comp, "I'll call him back and let him know you're coming, ok?"

"That'll be great, thanks Robert!" Wendy beamed, "I know Matthew's probably sitting right beside you, isn't he?"

"Oh…. uh, yeah." I stammered, "He is right here. Would you like to talk to him?"

"No." Wendy said flatly, "You just tell him to stay out of trouble for me, ok?"

I smiled to myself, "You got it, I'll give Sammy a call. It was nice talking to you again, and thanks for the favor. Take care."

"No problem." Wendy said, "You take care, too. And punch Matthew for me, ok? Bye-bye." Wendy hung up. I leaned over and punched Matt in the shoulder. He turned and glared at me.

I started laughing again as I dialed the house phone right next to the 8 Star entrance.

I glanced at the clock and noticed it was almost time for the Jester's Court escort. Hank was tied up. Even if he wasn't I wouldn't have sent him on the escort but it was still fun to think about. The last thing I wanted on my Friday would be a fight between Hank and Tom. I glanced down at my schedule to see who was available.

"Control to 278." No answer. I hated calling officers more than once. "Control to 278." Nothing. "Earth to 278, can you hear your radio?" I asked sarcastically.

"Go ahead, Control." Walter's bored voice finally answered.

"Jester's Court escort." I said grumpily.

"Copy, escort Tom to the Jester's Court." answered Walter, still sounding bored.

I looked over at Matt still pouting after my punch. "You know, this wouldn't be so bad if these guys would actually do what they're paid for." I said.

"It really wasn't my fault, you know!" Matt answered.

"What wasn't your fault?" I asked, confused.

"I like Wendy!" he continued, "But that other girl hit on me! What was I supposed to do?"

"Oh jeez, not this again!" I turned towards the monitors, "You need to let it go, Matt. I don't want to hear about Wendy for the rest of the night! Sheesh!"

"But I don't want to let it go!" Matt whined.

I sighed and started panning one of the monitors around, checking out the Cloud Nine Lounge. I stopped on a familiar looking young woman.

"Lookie who's here!" I said with a smile, pointing at the monitor.

"Who?" Matt asked, leaning forward to get a better look.

"Control to Lead Three." I said.

"Lead Three." Albert answered.

"Who are you looking at?" Matt asked, "The hooker?"

"Don't you recognize her?" I asked chuckling, "Lead Three, the female we 86'ed last night is back in the Cloud Nine Lounge."

"Ohhh!" Matt said, realizing at last, "It's Bunhilda or Brunheidi, or something like that, right?"

"Brunhilda." I corrected, "Yeah, the one who assaulted Jack."

"Send an officer," Albert replied, "And let's try to walk her out, ok?"

I looked at Matt shaking my head, "Copy Lead Three." I looked at my schedule happy I didn't have Jack to send, afraid he'd get spit on again. As I was looking, Cortez arrived at the lounge. He must have been close, or ran to the

lounge.

"501 to Control, I've got her," Cortez piped up, "I'll walk her out."
"Be careful, Cortez!" I cautioned, "We've had problems with this one!"

I watched the monitor as Cortez approached Brunhilda. It was like watching an

old black and white movie with no sound. The picture was color, but there was

no sound at all. Cortez pointed towards the front door and seemed to be chatting

with Brunhilda. I could almost hear piano music in my head. Cortez Domingo:

Chief of the Keystone Kops!

Brunhilda got up from the bar and started chatting away with Cortez. I started

to wonder if he was going to walk her out. Thankfully, after a minute she started

towards the main entrance as Cortez followed along. When they neared the door,

I switched to an outside camera. I waited for them to come out the door. Instead

of Cortez and Brunhilda, I saw more trouble.

The man from yesterday wearing what looked like a white bed sheet was at the

casino entrance waving a sign. He was screaming at everyone who walked by.

Cortez would be heading right for him. I thought to warn him and actually leaned

towards the microphone when Cortez and Brunhilda came out the door. The Bed

Sheet Man ran straight for them.

He started jabbing a finger at Cortez and tried to chase Brunhilda. She quickly

jumped in a cab and rode away. Losing the girl, the crazy man turned back on

Cortez.

I looked over my schedule for someone to back Cortez up.

"Control to 125!" I yelled into the radio. No answer. I tried again, "Control to 125!" I figured I'd better move up the chain of command as it looked like Cortez might need help.

"Control to Lead Two or Lead Three, we have a male dressed only in a bed sheet getting nasty with Cortez outside the main entrance. Could one of you respond?"

"501 to Control." came Cortez' voice. I could hear the man behind him yelling something like, "Sinner! You'll all pay for this!"

"Go ahead, 501." I responded, "And be advised, we have you up on camera." That would let him know I could see him on camera.

"This guy's 421!" Cortez continued, "He keeps screaming about how we're all sinners and making threats." "421" is the term we used for crazy.

"What kind of threats is he making?" I asked.

"Lead Two to Control," Walt finally responded, "Is someone making threats to someone else? What's going on?"

"Uh, that's what I was calling you guys for," I said, "We have a guy at the main entrance wearing a sheet, making threats. We need a supervisor out there."

"501 to Control," Cortez said, "I think he wants to burn down the hotel. He keeps on screaming about the *cleansing fire*."

"Lovely." I said, looking at Matt. "Lead Two, are you going to respond for this?"

"Affirmative." replied Walt," I'm on my way."
I tried again to call Stewart for some back up, "Control to 125!"

"125, go ahead," answered Stewart. A miracle.

"Head outside and back up 501 with the Sheet Guy." I instructed.

"Uh…yeah, Sheet Guy." Stewart repeated.

"Look," Matt said, starting to laugh, "He's got a little dance!" Sheet Guy had indeed started to dance around Cortez. Cortez didn't seem impressed and had a sour look on his face.

Stewart walked out the doors followed by Walt and Albert. Sheet Guy continued to dance around, ignoring the new arrivals. Walt and Albert seemed to be trying to talk to him, but he kept dancing and hopping around them.

"What do you suppose they're saying to him?" Matt asked.

"Probably asking him where he got his sheet." I said quietly, "Or if he'd like them to comp him a golf game, maybe."

"I don't think golf is healthy in a bed sheet." Matt replied.

I gave Matt a confused look. He smiled back and shrugged.

Walt eventually lost his patience and pointed at Sheet Guy. Cortez grabbed him; Stewart and Albert helped put Sheet Guy into cuffs.

"Lead Two to Control." Walt said, "We'll be taking one to the C.S.O. for harassing guests and staff. 421; roll the paramedics for him, Ok?"

"I'm going to need some info before I can roll." I started, "Approximately how old is he, and what is the problem?"

"I don't know how old he is," Walt sounded annoyed, "Just roll em'!"

"Once again, Sir!" I kept trying, "I can't roll paramedics without certain info. They simply won't come just because I tell them to roll. They'll want to know what the problem is."

"Ok: the *problem* is we have a man wearing nothing but a bed sheet screaming and not making any coherent sense! Now roll the paramedics and I'll call Metro from the C.S.O."

"Copy." I muttered. I looked over at Matt who was already on the phone with the paramedics. I glanced back at the monitor in time to see Sheet Guy step on part of his sheet as they walked him to the C.S.O. The sheet hit the floor. Now Stewart and Cortez were walking a completely naked man into the casino. Cortez stopped to pick up the sheet and Sheet Gut started struggling with Stewart. Cortez dropped the sheet and went back to help Stewart. Finally, after a minute or so they simply drug the naked man to the C.S.O. door and inside.

"Control to all units, we'll be going into thirty-three traffic for a medical emergency for the Sheet Man! No radio traffic unless absolutely necessary!" I announced.

"Make it hot!" Albert said and walked in the C.S.O. door. Matt pushed record on the V.C.R and turned up the volume so we could hear inside the room.

"Sinners! Sinners!" Sheet Guy was screaming, "The claw of the grand happy will flesh out the beans and sauce!"

I looked at Matt with a big smile on my face, "Did you hear that? The beans and sauce will be fleshed out!"

"What the hell?" Matt replied as we both watched the C.S.O. monitor. Albert had retrieved and brought the sheet with them, but Sheet Guy refused to cover himself with it now. He sat on the bench still cuffed, squirming, yelling, and completely naked. It was like watching a train wreck, you didn't really want to see it, but you couldn't quite turn away.

The phone rang four times before either of us noticed. Matt finally answered it. He talked to whoever it was for a minute, turned to me, and said something was going on at the 8 Star Club. They apparently were tossing someone out.

I looked over at the monitor showing the front of the 8 Star and saw Sammy chatting with Wendy. I was happy for the moment, until two large figures came out of the club from behind Sammy and tossed a woman onto the casino floor. She lay there, face down and not moving. The two figures walked back into the 8 Star as if nothing had happened.

I looked over at Matt, "Do you believe this shit?" I asked. "Control to…." I let go of the radio button and tried to think what unit was left and not busy on a call. Phil came to mind. The E.M.T. was always a good choice when someone was down. "Control to 191."

"191 go ahead." Phil answered the first time.

" Are you clear of the nightstand report? Can you please check on a down female they just tossed out of the 8 Star, ok? She is on the floor and not moving."

"They tossed her out and now she's not moving?" Phil asked.

"Yep, that's about the size of it." I answered. The phone started ringing again so Matt answered it. It looked like busy time was about to start.

I was starting at the monitor, waiting for Phil to arrive when Matt turned to me and said there was some kind of emergency in the Ambrosia Restaurant. *Phooey*! I thought, who do I call now? I guess I'd have to bring someone down from the hotel to help out on the floor.

"Control to 268." No response. Shirly was one I knew I might have to call several times. "Control to 268!" Nothing. I had to call her four times before she finally answered.

"Uh…268, I was talking to some people." Shirly's unsure voice replied.

"268 log off track and head to the Ambrosia. Some kind of disturbance call there, let me know what's going on, ok?"

Normally, I would send the R&S Officer. That was Walter and he was supposed to be on the Jester's Court escort. I was a bit short on units tonight and I hoped this wouldn't turn out to be a mistake.

The screaming continued from the C.S.O., "Sinners! Sinners! You'll all pay for delaying the major domo of society! I pass on that which needs to be passed on!"

I looked over at Matt, "We're starting to get a bit busy now, can you turn that back down?" Matt looked at me and turned down the volume.

Phil arrived at the front of the 8 Star and starting checking the woman on the floor. She still seemed lifeless, but more than likely just really drunk; hopefully not dead.

"191 to Control." came Phil with the explanation.

"Go ahead, 191." I couldn't wait to hear this. Or maybe, I could.

"She's breathing and has a heartbeat, but she's not conscious. We're gonna have to roll paramedics for possible alcohol poisoning. Female, early twenties, unconscious, but breathing."

"Oh for God's sake!" I screamed, "We're already in thirty–three traffic!" I pressed the radio button again, "Ok, we're rolling again. Control to all units, we're *still* in thirty-three traffic for a medical emergency in front of the 8 Star."

Matt was on the phone again to the paramedics. An ambulance pulled up to the front entrance as he was calling for the second time. Albert was outside to meet them. He greeted the paramedics, called in their ambulance number to me, and led them into the C.S.O.

"Are you going to clear thirty-three?" Matt asked.

"Not yet," I replied, "We're still waiting for the paramedics for Phil!

Remember, the one you just called for?"

"Oh yeah!" Matt smiled, "I was too wrapped up in Mr. Sheet Guy, I guess."

He smiled and I chuckled back at him.

While waiting for the second ambulance we watched the C.S.O. monitor. The

paramedics walked in and one greeted Sheet Guy. "Hey, Moses! When did you

get out and what are you doing here bothering these nice people?"

"You don't know me!" Moses screamed back at him, "You're another sinner

who doesn't know about the cake mix!"

"They don't know about the *cake mix*!" I repeated to Matt, laughing.

"Calm down, Moses." the paramedic said, "What happened to your clothes?"

Matt answered the ringing phone. The phones continued to ring and I noticed

another call from the Jester's Court. I picked up the phone, "Security, this is

Robert."

"Hi Robert, this is Will James, Manager of Jester's Court. I need to find out

why you haven't escorted Tom down to the theater yet."

"Why I haven't…." I started, "I sent someone on that escort an hour ago!"

"Well, they never arrived!" Will said angrily, "We need to start the show and

Tom's not here! He's been calling me about the escort!"

"I'm sorry, Sir," I said, "I'll find out what happened and get someone up there

for the escort right now."

"Well, you'd better get on the ball!" Will said nastily, "I'll be speaking to your supervisor about you people not doing your jobs!" He hung up, and I wasn't very happy.

Before I could explode over the radio at Walter, Matt turned to me, "That was Shirly in the Ambrosia. Someone hit her with a pie."

"Walter didn't…" I started, "Did you just say someone hit Shirly with a *pie*?"

"Yeah," Matt continued, "She said there was another food fight going on in there. When she arrived someone hit her with a pie."

"Did she take them into custody?" I asked as the phone began to ring again.

Matt answered the phone and put the person on hold and said it was for me. I answered the line tentatively, "Security, this is Robert."

"*Robair*!" screamed a voice I knew only too well, "Zis place is a zoo! A farking *zoo*! We need ze elp and you send ze lady who now is wearing ze pie! *Ze French Vanilla pie*!"

"Calm down Henry," I said, "What is going on there, is everything under control?"

"I vill not cook for animals!" Henry yelled back, "Ze pie vas a masterpiece! And now the lady wears it like a mask! How can I cook for zis kind of people? Why are you not here to help?"

"Henry? Henry, just listen a minute!" I screamed trying to calm him, "I'm positive not everyone in the restaurant was a part of the incident! Just because a few idiots caused some problems is no reason to deny good people your work,

ok?"

"Vhat good people?" Henry screamed, "Ze *pie*, ze *pie!*"

I felt my night quickly unraveling. Henry continued to scream at me on the phone and the paramedics were now trying to strap Moses, or Sheet Guy, or whoever he was to a gurney. He continued to scream at them that they were sinners; Walter hadn't shown up for the Jester's Court escort and now the show would be late. A pie had been thrown at Shirly. While all of this was going on an odd thought occurred to me: If I could just have the paramedics wheel Sheet Guy Moses over to explain to Henry about the cake mix, everything would be fine.

Finally, I hit my stress point. "Act like an adult, and a mature Chef!" I berated Henry over the phone, "Stop sweating one pie, we do the best we can and call me if someone else has a heart attack or a real emergency comes up! I slammed down the phone, picked the receiver back up, and dialed the C.S.O. Walt answered so I started in on him, "Tell that naked fuck to shut the hell up! And you might want to have a talk with Walter; he was assigned the Jester's Court escort over an hour ago and hasn't bothered to show up! Now the show's late and the manager's mad! No, don't ask me where he is, because I don't know or care!" I slammed down the phone and glared at Matt. "I've had enough!" I yelled, "I'm going to take a shit, I'll be back in a few minutes!" I got up and stormed out the door.

I walked into the bathroom and entered a stall. I sat down on the toilet without even pulling down my pants. It was nice to have a minute to breathe, a few seconds of quiet. I sat there and stared at the stall door. The image of Matt trying to answer phones with both hands and put things out over the radio at the same time crossed my mind and I felt a bit guilty. There were times when Matt and Paul had melted down in dispatch, too. It had a way of wearing on you. It wasn't being busy, it always seemed to be about some idiots not listening to what they were dispatched to do, or not going somewhere they were supposed to go. I got up out of the stall, went over to the sink and splashed some water on my face. I took a look at myself in the mirror and then headed back to dispatch. As I was coming down the hall I saw Paul wheeling his bike along going towards dispatch.

"What're you doing inside?" I asked.

"I guess it was your turn for a meltdown, huh?" Paul said smiling, "You ran off, so Matthew called me in to take your place because things are a bit busy right now."

"I've had it with these people." I explained, "I'm getting yelled at by managers because the idiots on the floor either can't handle themselves, or don't bother to show up for details!"

"I told you to transfer to bikes." Paul chuckled, "You won't have to worry about any of that shit when you're outside with us."

"Right," I said as we arrived at the dispatch door, "And you aren't being pulled into dispatch right now, are you?"

We opened the door and found Matt on the phone with many lines ringing. I walked back over to my chair, plopped down, and answered the phone, "Security, this is Robert."

"Yeah Robert, I thought I told you to get someone on Tom's escort!" came an angry voice, "I need to get this show started, and we don't need delays because of stupid security!"

"Hold, Please." I said punching the hold button. I looked over at both Matt and Paul, "Do you believe that fuck Walter still hasn't shown up for the Jester's Court escort?"

"Oh, Walt wants to talk to you about that," Matt said, "He called back just after you left wanting to know what was going on out here."

"Where is he now?" I asked.

"I don't know," Matt said, "They just left the C.S.O."

Paul picked up the phone and punched the line I had just put on hold, "Security, this is Paul!" he shouted into the phone. After a minute of listening to the angry voice scream, Paul said, "Don't sweat it, the show isn't that good, anyway." He hung up.

I began to laugh. Just that little bit of nastiness cheered me up. "He's…he's going to call Walt or somebody now." I choked out.

"Do I look like I care who he calls?" Paul said with a smile, "If he wants to yell at me, I can go down to his shitty, little theater and meet him in person!"

Matt seemed a bit cheered up by Paul, too. "I had to put out two lockouts and a noise complaint while you were gone. Not to mention the nasty call back I got from Walt after you called and screamed at him."

"Sorry," I said, "It's been a rough week and I just needed a quick break."

I pushed the radio button, "Control to Lead Two." No response; I called again, "Control to Lead Two!"

"Lead Two, go ahead." came Walt's voice. He sounded a bit annoyed. Good.

"Give me a call when you're free, please." I said nicely.

The phone was ringing less than ten seconds later. I picked it up and answered nicely, "Security, this is Robert."

"What is going on out there?" screamed Walt.

"A better question might be; What is going on in there?" I fired back. "I have a disturbance in the Ambrosia: the officer who responds gets hit by a pie and then walks away. The manager from the Jester's Court keeps calling me yelling about how he can't start the show because Walter doesn't bother to show up for Tom's escort, and both managers are in the C.S.O. with some screaming, naked man!"

"Well, you need to notify us about these things, not just run off." Walt said.

"Fine, you're being notified now!" I chirped. I could hear the unhappiness in my voice, "I still don't know where Walter is. Do we now just do whatever we feel like and not what we're dispatched to do?"

"The supervisors will handle this." Walt said, "For now, find out where Walter is and send him on the escort again, ok? And what was that about the Ambrosia?"

"I don't know!" I said getting a bit excited, "I was told there was a disturbance there and then a mad Chef calls me screaming about how someone hit the officer with a pie!"

"What did the Shirly say?" Walt asked.

"*Nothing*!" I yelled, "Shirly hasn't bothered to call in yet! She called my partner on a landline and told him she was hit by a pie, but that's all she said! I guess she doesn't even know who hit her!"

"So what's going on at the Ambrosia right now?" Walt asked.

"How the hell should I know?" I bellowed, "Maybe it's a Three Stooges marathon? Maybe Moe is over there directing her, because she certainly isn't being directed by me! All I can tell you is they're short one pie now!"

"You need to call these people and keep better track of them." Walt said

"So what you want, is for me to send someone on an escort, and then keep calling them every few minutes because there aren't any responsible adults in this department who can handle their own calls, right?"

"No, that's not what I said!" Walt backpedaled, "You just need to keep better track of where these people are!"

"Look," I said, "It's been a long week for me. Now I'm dealing with managers and Chefs calling me up and yelling at me for things that aren't my fault. I've just had enough, ok? I'm ready for my days off, I need to unwind."

"We've all had a tough week," Walt pushed, "It comes with the job."

"Yeeeeeaaaaaaaaah," I said, dragging the word out, "I've gotta go, it's getting busy again and I need to try and find Walter." I hung up the phone.
I looked at both Paul and Matt, "That just pissed me off more, you know?"

"Screw him!" Paul said.

"Control to 278." I ventured into the radio. Of course, no answer. I tried again, "Control to 278." I tried five more times with no response.

"Lead Two to 278." came Walt's voice over the radio. There was still no answer. "Lead Two to Control, put someone else on the escort and have Walter come and see me when you locate him, ok?"

"No problem," I answered, "Control to 156, are you available?"

"156 go ahead." A voice whispered. 156 was a quiet officer named Larry. He was somewhat reliable, but usually stayed in the hotel and didn't get involved in much.

"156, Log off track and do the Jester's Court escort, ok? And put a hustle on it because we're late and holding up the show."

"I've...I've never done that before." Larry's timid voice replied. I looked at both Matt and Paul. Paul was howling. "Give my partner a call and he'll explain what you have to do." I said to Larry.

"How do I get back outside?" Paul asked me, still giggling, "And where do I go when I get there? I've never been here before, what goes on here every night?"

I let a little chuckle escape me. I looked over at Matt, "So what did happen at the Ambrosia? And where is Shirly?"

"She got hit by a pie." Matt said, "And that's all she said when she called."

"She was hit by a pie." I repeated, "Did the pie fall out of the sky? Was the pie thrown? Where did the pie come from?"

"From the Ambrosia!" Paul answered as he went off in gales of laughter.

"I don't know." Matt answered, "I guess from the Ambrosia, like Paul says. All she said when she called was that she had been hit by a pie."

"Who the hell *are* you people?" I asked, "Why is it so hard for these people to do *anything*?"

Paul continued to laugh away. He got up and walked to the dispatch door, "If you ladies have things under control, I'm going to head to lunch. I'll come back after I get a sandwich or something, ok?"

"I can't leave, but bring me a fucking pie, ok?" I said glaring at Paul.

"From…from the Employee Dining Room?" Paul asked in between giggles.

"No, from the fucking sky!" I answered, "Or maybe the Ambrosia, wherever they're coming from right now. *Ze pie, ze pie!*" I tried to imitate Henry. Paul laughed so hard he had to sit down again.

"723 to Control." Hank drawled over the radio. It had been almost two hours since he had been sent on the guest complaint.

"Go ahead, 723." I said into the radio.

"Ok, I'm clear of room 6014," Hank said, "They don't want a report; they just wanted to tell somebody what happened."

I looked at Matt, "You've been up there listening to what happened for almost two hours! You should have sent them to the Front Desk or something!"

"Well…" Hank said and then hesitated, "They just wanted to talk to somebody and was up there to listen to them."

"Yes, I know why you were sent up there," I said, trying to be patient, "I'm the one who sent you up there. So they don't want a report now, right?"

"No, no report," Hank repeated himself again, "They just wanted to tell somebody…"

I looked at Matt, "Didn't they tell *you* over the phone? They just wanted to tell somebody, but telling *you* wasn't good enough!"

"What? Who told me something on the phone?" Matt asked confused.

"Go to lunch, 723." I said to Hank

The phones were ringing again. I couldn't wait for the shift to end. Matt answered one line, I answered another, "Security, this is Robert."

"Robair!" came the familiar voice, "I know you are ze busy, but I want to call and tell you I am sorry for you aving to yell at me. I get carried away about ze food sometimes."

"Not a problem, Henry." I said feeling a bit bad now, "I shouldn't have yelled at you in the first place. Things got a bit hectic in here and I took part of it out on you. I am sorry for yelling."

"You do ze hard job, oui?" Henry said, "And sometimes the hard job makes you mad and yell, oui? It's no problem; I just didn't want you to stay mad at me."

I could see another line ringing, but didn't want to insult Henry by just brushing him off, "I'm over it, Henry. I'm still a bit busy out here, but I'll stop by Ambrosia and say hello next week, ok? When I'm on the floor? I'll come by if I have time."

"Very good!" Henry shouted, I was watching the lights on the phone flash, "I am always appy to see you! You come by and maybe I make *you* ze very good pie!"

"Lovely, really lovely." I said, "I've got lines ringing right now, I do have to go. I'll see you later, Henry." I hung up and answered another line:

"Security, this is Robert."

"Uh yeah…hi…" a hesitant voice said, "Do you have ghosts in this hotel?"

"Do we have ghosts?" I repeated, "I don't know where you would get a ghost from. Why would you want a ghost, anyway?"

"We don't *want* any ghosts, but there are some up here." the person said.

"There are ghosts up there?" I repeated again. I looked at the caller ID and saw this was coming from the very top floor, room 52001, "Are the ghost disturbing you, keeping you awake, taking your stuff?"

"Well, they are bothering us," the man said, "Can you hear that?" There was a pause as I was supposed to hear something. I didn't hear a thing. "Can you hear that? What *is* that? It's scaring my wife and I need the ghosts to stop, ok?"

"I'll tell you what, Sir," I said, "I'll send up an officer and he can check into what you're hearing, ok? Is it ok for the officer to knock on your door and you let him hear the noise?"

"Whatever makes it stop." he said and hung up.

"I don't believe this place, sometimes, "I said to Matt, "What have you got for me? What were your fun phone calls?"

"Oh... uh," Matt hesitated as he looked at his notepad so he wouldn't forget anything, "Phil's done with his report and the girl was transported while you were in the bathroom. Phil went to lunch and guess who he found in the lunch room?"

"Let me guess," I said sourly, "Walter was down there eating, right?"

"Actually, no." Matt said, "He's down there asleep with his head down on a table. I already called Walt and he says he'll deal with it."

"What's he going to do?" I asked, "He always says he'll deal with it! Maybe he will sleep next to him? Sheesh."

"Yeah, I know," Matt continued, "Next, I have a few people calling from the top floor in the big tower upset about the noise the wind is making up there. I forwarded them to the front desk."

"The wind!" I said, realizing what the ghosts had to be, "Some guy just called me about ghosts on fifty-two! I should probably call him back, but I think I'll send an officer anyway."

"Yeah," Matt continued, "Well, you can send Shirly if you want now. She called and said she cleaned the pie off her face. She got another uniform from wardrobe and is now back up in the tower."

"She cleaned the pie off her face…" I said, stunned, "Did she mention what happened at the Ambrosia at all?"

"You know, I asked about that this time." Matt said, "She told me there were some people throwing food. One of them hit her in the face with the pie and she ran away."

"She ran away?!" I said, getting upset again, "She didn't call for back up, tell us what was going on, or even confront the food throwers? She just ran away?"

"Yup, I guess so." Matt said.

"So it doesn't matter to her what people do as long as she can run away from it, huh?" I screamed, "Are things ok at the Ambrosia? Did the food throwing stop?"

"I don't know," Matt said, "I guess we should check on that, huh?"

I picked up a receiver and dialed the number for Ambrosia. A tired sounding lady answered, "Thank you for calling the Ambrosia, this is Ariana."

"Hi Ariana," I said nicely, "It's Robert from Security. You sound really tired, I guess it's been a rough night all around, huh?"

"I've been here for two food fights tonight," Ariana said, "I'm pretty sick of this place right now."

"I'll bet you are," I said with a little chuckle, "We've been pretty busy here in dispatch and all I got from the officer I sent for the last food fight was that she was hit by a pie. Is everything ok there?"

"Yes, for now everything is calm." Ariana answered. That was just what I wanted to hear, "Things calmed down after the pie was thrown. It was a couple of hotel guests who were just a little drunk. They paid for the pie and left."

"Did they tear up the restaurant?" I asked.

"No, no, no!" Ariana explained, "It was just a little food fight in a booth. It was just three guys, not the whole restaurant. What kind of a place do you think we run here?"

"Chef Henry called me up all upset, and I thought it was some kind of huge deal." I said.

"Henry's always upset!" Ariana chuckled, "That's just his way. He spends all night screaming in French at the other chefs in the kitchen."

"I see," I said, relieved, "I just needed to make sure everything was under control. Thanks Ariana."

"You can count on us to maintain control here." Ariana said with a laugh, "It's borderline control, but still control. Thanks for calling, Robert. Good-bye." She hung up the phone and I felt better.

I turned to Matt, "It was three guys in a booth. No huge food fight, no big problem, just three drunks in a booth!"

"Three Stooges, maybe?" Matt asked.

"Yes," I confirmed, "The Three Stooges hit Shirly with a pie. Welcome to Paradise!"

I pressed the radio button, "Control to 268."

"268, Go ahead. I'm pie-free now." Shirly's voice beamed. I turned to Matt and gave him a sour look.

"268, head up to the top floor in the main tower and check on a complaint of ghosts making noise."

"Check on…. on…. they're making…." Shirly answered uncertainly.

"Yes," I said into the radio, "Check on a complaint of ghosts making too much noise. If you can't hear anything, make contact with room 52001 and he'll introduce you to the ghosts."

Shirly pushed her radio button, but didn't talk for a few seconds. We could hear her breathing, almost like an obscene phone call on the radio. Finally, she said, "Copy."

Matt turned to me and told me Larry was on hold waiting to talk to me. I picked up the phone, "Yeah Larry, what is it?"

"I did that escort," He said sounding uncertain, "And it went ok, but the guy, Tom or whatever his name is, kept throwing confetti at me!"

I looked over at Matt with a crooked smile on my face, "Really? Confetti? Where did he get confetti from? How odd is that?"

"He had this bag!" Larry continued, "And he kept pulling it from there! Anyway, he's in the theater and they started the show. People were upset, but he's down there now."

"Great job, Larry." I said, "Confetti or not, you did good. I'm glad the show is going on. Let me know when you're back on track, Ok?"

"Yeah, ok," Larry said, still sounding unsure of himself, "But don't you think that's odd? That he would throw confetti at me like that? Who's going to clean that up?"

"I dunno, Larry," I answered, "I just dunno. You feel free to go back on track, though." I hung up on Larry.

"Tom threw confetti at Larry." I said to Matt.

"Imagine that!" Matt said in a quiet monotone, "Terrible Tom throwing confetti! What could happen next, maybe the Three Stooges will hit someone with a pie? Oh wait, we've already had that, too!"

"Don't forget the ghosts!" I added, "I sent Shirly on the ghost call!"

The dispatch door opened and in walked Paul. "Hello ladies! Here's your pie, Robair!" He set a plate with a large slice of chocolate cream pie down in front of me. "Please don't throw it at Shirly."

I scooped up a small bit of the pie and threw it behind me at the wall. It made a small splat and started to slide slowly down the wall. "How's that?" I said to

Paul, "That wasn't at Shirly. Are we happy now?"

"Ecstatic!" Paul answered, laughing. He leaned across me and pressed my

radio button, "Whooooooooooooooo!" he howled.
"What the hell are you doing?" I asked laughing.

"Ambiance." Paul said, "Just setting the mood for Shirly."

"The phone rang yet again and Matt answered it. I looked down and noticed it

was the Security Booth this time.

"So, Robair," Paul said putting his feet up on the table and started eating a large

sandwich, "Lots of stress tonight, huh? People getting to you?"

"That food fight incident in the Ambrosia was three drunk guys in a booth.

They hit Shirly with a pie and she ran away." I said.

"Three drunks, huh?" Paul asked, "Maybe we should change the name of the

restaurant to that? The Three Drunks?"

"Lovely, just lovely." I said, "I'm sure Henry would just love that."

"Oh yes!" Paul said, "Your pet chef!"

Matt put the phone on hold and said it was for me again. I looked up at the

booth monitor and saw Jerry holding the phone to his ear. "Yeah Jerry," I said,

picking up the receiver, "What do you need?"

"See this guy in front of me?" Jerry asked, "He wants a report done because

he's missing a shoe."

"He's missing his shoes?" I asked, "Are they missing from his room?"

"No, shoe singular." Jerry said, "He's missing one shoe. The other one's still on his foot."

I didn't know what to say, I looked over at Paul. "He's missing one shoe. From his foot?" I asked.

"Yeah, he thinks so." Jerry explained, "But he's pretty drunk and doesn't know how long the shoe has even been off his foot."

"And he wants a report over this?" I asked.

"Yes, he'd like a report done." Jerry said.

"Why do you call me with this kind of shit? I asked, "Are you kidding me? You want me to send an officer to do a report because some drunk's shoe fell off somewhere?"

"I've already tried to explain to him…." Jerry started.

"No." I interrupted, "We aren't doing a report because a drunk is missing a shoe! Tell him to go away!"

"Hey, don't you think I've tried?" Jerry said, "I've been dealing with this log for quite a while now! He won't leave! Can you at least send me someone to move him along? Help get him away from the booth?"

I sighed, "Yeah, give me a minute, I'll send someone over." I hung up the phone and pushed the radio button, "Control to 501."

It took about 15 seconds to get an answer, and it was a long 15 seconds, "501, go ahead."

"Head over to the booth and help Jerry remove a log." I said.

"A log?" Cortez asked, "You need me to help him move a log?"

"You should let sleeping logs lie." Paul said, still munching on his sandwich. "Leave Walter out of this!" I said sarcastically. Paul started to laugh and almost choked on his sandwich.

"Affirm," I said into the radio, "Head over to the booth and help out Jerry with the log."

The phone rang. It was from the manager's office. I grabbed the phone receiver before Matt and answered, "Security, this is Robert!"

"Yeah, Robert," came Albert's voice, "What's all this about a log at the booth?"

"Jerry wants a log to move on," I explained, "It won't leave and it's bothering him."

"A log?" Albert asked, "What do you mean a log is bothering him?"

"Did you people take care of Walter?" I asked, "Did you even do anything to him? Or is it not a problem to skip doing details you don't like?"

"Talk to Walter?" Albert asked, "Skip doing…what *are* you talking about?"

"I knew it!" I screamed, "You guys didn't do anything, did you?"

"I don't know what you're talking about." Albert started backpedaling. I had him on the run now.

"Yes, you do." I said plainly, "Walt said he was going to talk to Walter about not bothering to do the Jester's Court escort and making the show start late! You're a manager, too! Shouldn't you be talking to him also?"

"If Walt told you…" Albert started.
"Sorry, got to go! I've got other calls coming in!" I hung up.

"What was that all about?" Paul asked.

"Just screwing with Albert." I said, "Walter didn't do the escort and the show was late. The manager called me up screaming just before I walked out. So I called and yelled at Walt."

"Yes, I was here when you called Walt." Paul said.

"So I thought it was Walt when I saw the call was from the office. But, it's just as much fun to screw with Albert. He's as confused as ever."

I turned and looked at the monitors. I was only half way through the shift and I was ready to leave. Some nights were like that.

"268 to Control?" Shirly's voice came through the radio like a question.

"Yeah, go ahead 268." I answered back.

"I couldn't hear anything up here, so I made contact with 52001." Shirly always sounded so unsure of everything, "I think it's the wind making the noise. What do I do?"

"Tell the wind to be quiet." I said simply.

"Don't be silly!" Shirly giggled back, "You know I can't do that! I'm serious, what should I do about the noise?"

I looked at Paul, and then over at Matt. "I'm completely stumped here. What should she do?"

"Well, my lunch is finished." Paul answered, "And while I'd love to sit and debate what Shirly should do about the wind, I have to get back outside. Call me when you get mad and run off again!"

"Lovely." I said, as Paul walked out the dispatch door. I pushed the transmit button again, "If there's nothing you can do about the noise, have him call the front desk for a room change, or something."

"But, he likes this room." Shirly answered.

"Well then, the ghosts win!" I said sarcastically. I figured one of the managers would call me and tell me to lay off the sarcasm again, but that didn't happen.

"501 to Control." Cortez piped up. I looked up at the booth monitor and saw him standing there.

"Go ahead, 501." I answered, knowing I probably wasn't going to like what he had to say.

"Yeah, this guy wants a report," Cortez said, "He's missing some stuff."

"Some stuff…" I answered, "And what *stuff* is he missing?"

"He says his shoe is gone. And he's missing other stuff, too!" Cortez said.

I shook my head and looked at Matt, who smiled back at me. "Ok, once again: What other *stuff* is he missing?"

"Well, he's pretty drunk." Cortez answered, "He doesn't know, he wants us to check the cameras to see what stuff he's missing."

"Check what cameras?" I asked, playing along.

"You know!" Cortez insisted, "The casino cameras! He wants us to check and see where his shoe went, and what else he's missing."

"Ok, let me ask you this." I kept playing, "How does this guy even know cameras were watching him?"

"He says he's seen the movies." Cortez said, not seeming to understand, "And he knows we're watching him."

"Is this guy a hotel guest?" I finally asked.

"I don't know." Cortez answered.

"How about you ask him?" I said, now starting to get aggravated.

Cortez finally answered after a minute of talking to the man. "He says he is, but he doesn't have a room key and won't tell me his room number."

"How about ID?" I asked, "Does this guy have any ID?"

Cortez spoke with the man some more. A couple of times it looked like the man was going to fall over. It was almost like watching a silent movie. "Nope. He says it's gone, too."

"Ok, how about a name?" I asked, "Can we at least get his name?"

"He doesn't want to tell me his name." Cortez said, "He just wants the report and says he wants to see the tapes, too."

"What tapes?" I asked.

"The tapes from the cameras, don't be stupid!" Cortez said.

"Landline, please." I said nicely.

I watched the monitor as Jerry dialed the phone and handed the receiver to Cortez. I answered before the first ring even finished. "You tell this drunken idiot to get lost!" I screamed, "He wants to make demands, but won't give his name and doesn't have ID." Tell him to piss off!"

"But he's missing…" Cortez started.

"Show him the door!" I said angrily, "We aren't going to play with this drunken moron anymore! If he's actually missing something, tell him to come back when he's sober, ok?" I hung up the phone.

Cortez didn't hang up his receiver. Instead, he reached over the booth and dialed another number. He was calling a supervisor. Lovely.

We watched him chat on the phone for a few minutes and then hang up. The phone in dispatch rang. Matt answered and said it was Walt for me.

"Security, this is Robert." I said nicely.

"Ah Robert, do we have a missing property up at the booth?" Walt asked.

"No," I answered, "We have a drunk with no ID, who won't give his name, and keeps demanding to see camera coverage to find the shoe he lost."

"But he's missing other things, right?" Walt asked, "Not just a shoe?"

"I dunno." I answered, "He won't say. I'm being told he keeps demanding to see coverage. He says he'll find out if he's missing anything when he sees the mysterious *casino tapes*!"

"What is this about tapes?" Walt asked.

"Hey, feel free to head to the booth and speak with this guy if you want." I said, "You'd better hurry though, it looks like he's going to fall down soon."

"He's that drunk?" Walt asked.

"You know, I do know what I'm doing out here." I said simply, "Just because Cortez calls you and says he doesn't want to do what I told him to do doesn't mean I don't know what I'm doing!"

"Well…ah…he was just checking with us." Walt tried to explain.

"Did you talk to Walter?" I asked, "Did you go down to the dining area and drag him off a table?"

"Yes, I spoke with Walter," Walt said, "We're dealing with the situation. Don't worry about that!" *Sure you are,* I thought to myself.

"Well then, I guess either you can visit the booth and toss this guy," I suggested, "Or you can call the booth and tell Cortez to do what he was told in the first place."

"Yeah, I'll give him a call." Walt said, "But make a log entry for this. When he comes back later saying we wouldn't help him, we need documentation that we at least tried."

"We didn't try." I said, "He wouldn't give a name or show ID. He just kept making demands, so we tossed him out."

"Well make an entry anyway!" Walt said and hung up the phone.

I looked down at the log sheet in front of me. What should I write? *It's been a rough night tonight,* I thought to myself, *I'll just write something stupid. Nobody reads these things, anyway.* I wrote, "Stupid man missing a shoe will not leave Security Booth. Cortez sent and calls Walt. Per Lead Two everybody happy with just a log entry.

I looked up at the monitor and saw Cortez on the phone. He nodded his head a few times, as if whoever he was talking to could see him. He hung up and started talking to the drunk man once again.

The man started waving his arms around and then fell onto the floor. Cortez leaned down as if to help the man up. He backed away as the man started getting up on his own screaming. It was like watching an old Charlie Chaplin movie. Or better yet, like I always say to myself, The Keystone Cops. We moved the camera and watched for a bit as Cortez herded the man away from the booth.

"Control to 501."

After a pause, "501 go ahead."

"Is this guy leaving?" I asked, "What door is he going out? Or is he going up to a room?"

"He says he's going to play in the casino." Cortez answered, "So I just let him walk away."

I smiled and laughed, looking over at Matt, "Oooo, the fun never stops in Paradise, does it?" Matt gave me a sour look back.

"Any more calls?" I asked, "Any more emergencies to aggravate me and make me run off again?"

"For the moment it's quiet." Matt said blandly.

I leaned back in my chair and put my feet up on the table just like Paul did during his little visit. It was nice to relax for a bit. I didn't figure it would last, but I could be comfortable for a few minutes.

"268 to Control." Shirly squeaked over the radio.

"Yahoo!" I exclaimed to Matt, "Another Shirly call! I wonder if the guy in 52001 hit her with a pie this time?" Matt gave me a polite chuckle. "Go ahead, 268! What's the haps now?"

"I talked to the front desk and they said they would comp the room because of the noise. I talked to the guest and he was happy about that."

"You mean the ghost noise?" I asked.

"Affirmative." Shirly came back, "Everything's taken care of. I'll let you know when I'm back tracking the hotel."

"Fabulous!" I screamed into the microphone! I looked over at Matt, "She took care of everything! Don't you feel safer now?"

"You're sure all hopped up at the moment." Matt said.

"Oh, just looking at the clock and counting down the hours until days off! I'm certainly ready for them this week!"

Matt looked up at the clock, "Yeah, two more hours, yahoo."

"It goes by pretty fast when you get kind of busy, doesn't it?" I asked,

"Especially the few minutes when I left dispatch! I'm betting that's what you're all grumpy about, am I right?"

"Kind of," Matt said, "I volunteered for some overtime tomorrow, so I'll be working. I'm a bit bummed about that now. I kind of wish I hadn't volunteered."

"So tell Walt you changed your mind." I suggested.

"I can't do that," Matt said, "Because of vacations he really needs a dispatcher, and he went on and on about it until I said I'd come in."

"That dirty old man!" I screamed, "Let me teach you a new word, Matthew! No! Its spelled N-O. It's a fabulous word and you should try it out sometime!"

"You could come in and work dispatch with me!" Matt suggested back.

"After the week I had?" I smiled, "Not a chance. But you have fun! I'll think about you while I'm sipping a Pina Colada on a tropical island."

"You're going out drinking?" Matt asked, "Really? Maybe I should try to get out of working."

"Absolutely not!" I said decisively, "You volunteered, they need someone, done deal!" I started to laugh and the phone started ringing.

Matt answered; after a minute of talking to someone turned to me and said, "We've got a major problem in room 2624, possible rape."

"Suspect still up there?" I asked.

"Negative," Matt said picking up the phone automatically to call a supervisor, "Victim is in the room with a friend."

I leaned into the radio and pushed the transmit button, "Control to 111." I might not get along with Jack, but I was certain he'd handle things better than most.

"111 go ahead." he replied. It was near the end of the shift and he sounded tired. Sometimes a shift would take the energy right out of you, busy or not.

"Start heading to room 2624 for a possible sexual assault. No suspect description as of yet, but the victim is up there. I'll get you a female officer."

"Copy, give me the room number again." Jack answered.

"2624 get a move on! A supervisor should also be enroute and will meet you up there." I looked over at Matt to confirm this, and he nodded back while on the phone.

I could feel tension creeping into my spine and even maybe a little excitement. "Control to 268." Shirly was not my first choice, but she was the only available female officer.

No response, so I tried again; "Control to 268!" I hated people not answering me when I really needed them. I tried again, "Control to 268!" There was still no response.

"126 to Control." another female voice spoke up, "I'm available and can go up on this call if you need me." This officer was named Sheila. She was supposed

to be at the podium in front of the tower elevator.

"I can't have you leave your post 126, but thanks for the offer." I said, wishing

I could send her.

"It's ok; Larry's here and can take my place while you need me." she said.

Sheila was another quiet officer who liked to stay up in the hotel usually. I was

really glad of her help right now, though.

"Copy 126, head up." I said relieved, "The room number is 2624. And thanks

156, great teamwork!"

Now all I could do was sit back and wait. After a minute, Jack called in that he

and Walt had arrived at room 2624. We waited for more information, which as

dispatchers was all we really could do.

Soon, the phone rang. Matt answered it. It was Walt telling us to notify the

police and to send someone *reliable* to check the Cloud Nine Lounge for a suspect

matching the description he was going to give.

"Reliable?" I asked Matt, "Who the hell does he want me to send?"

"I don't know," Matt answered, "He just said someone reliable."

"Lovely." I said almost to myself, "Welcome to Paradise." I pushed transmit,

"Control to 191." I figured Phil was reliable.

"191, go ahead Control." Phil answered.

"Head over to the Cloud Nine and see if you can find…" I paused and looked over at Matt for the description. He had it written down on a small piece of paper and passed it over to me, "You're looking for a white male adult wearing jeans, a white shirt, and possible a red baseball cap. His name is John Presley."

"Uh… I'm up in 2624, Control." Phil said, "I came up here when the call first came out."

I shook my head and looked at Matt. "Unbelievable." I said. "Control to 723, are you still on the floor, or did you go up to the room, too?"

"723 to Control, I'm still on the floor." Hank's voice echoed, "Can you give me the description again?"

"Break!" Walter interrupted, "I have Mr. Presley here at the lounge. He's going to leave, though."

"Head over there, Hank!" I yelled into the radio, "No, he's not going to leave!"

"Metro's rolled the paramedics." Matt said, ignoring the radio traffic.

I leaned over the camera controls and brought up what I could see of the lounge. I just caught a glimpse of Walter following a guy in a white shirt towards the main entrance.

"278 stop that guy!" I yelled, "Put him in restraints if you have to, but he needs to stop!"

"He says he didn't do anything wrong and he's going to leave." Walter said. I switched to a camera at the front entrance and watched as the man walked out the door.

"Stop him Walter!" I screamed again, "Stop him, he's a suspect in a felony, you need to stop him!"

"Yeah, but he says…" Walter droned. The man walked over to the cab line.

I started to panic now. Someone needed to stop this guy! Just then, Hank came running out the entrance and pushed Walter aside. He walked up to the man and pointed back into the casino. The man hesitated and then started to scream at Hank. Hank started to scream back and the man pushed him. Hank grabbed him and threw him into a nearby wall. When the man hit the wall, Hank grabbed him again and threw him down onto the ground. It was like watching a rag doll being tossed around! The man hit the ground and Hank was immediately on top of him, trying to put on handcuffs. Cortez came running out the door and began to help Hank.

Once he was cuffed, Hank pulled the man to his feet. Hank and Cortez took him back inside the casino towards the C.S.O. "One male in restraints going to the C.S.O." Hank said into his radio, "Get ready to go hot!"

They arrived at the C.S.O. Walter opened the door for them. When they walked by, Hank stopped in the doorway and gave Walter a really nasty look. Walter followed them inside. Matt pushed the record button and we listened to a really angry Hank.

"You get the hell out of here!" He screamed at Walter, "You didn't help at all! You can't even be bothered to back up another officer!"

Possibly remembering the other day when he hadn't helped Matt with a fight, Cortez shifted his feet and looked at the floor.

"Hey, you don't need to get so mad," Walter said, "He said he didn't do anything,"

"OUT!" Hank screamed, and Walter walked out the door. "Put him up against the wall and check him for weapons." Hank said to Cortez as he sat down behind the desk.

"Bike Three to Control," came Paul's voice, "Paramedics on property. Where would you like them to go?"

"Oh…uh, take them up to room 2624, that's where the victim is, ok?" I answered.

"No problem." Paul said.

"Do you believe Walter didn't stop that guy?" I asked Matt.

"Remember that fight the other day?" Matt said, "When Cortez didn't help me at all either?"

I nodded, "What the hell happened to this place? Sheesh."

Shortly, a police cruiser pulled up next to the ambulance parked out front. I called Cortez in the C.S.O. and directed him to go and get the police officer. He escorted him up to the room to talk to the victim.

"Another exciting night, huh?" I asked Matt smiling.

"I think I need another no-lunch." Matt said, sounding really tired.

Time went by really quickly with all the action. We had about a half an hour to go. The police officer hadn't come down from the room yet to talk to the suspect. Everything seemed to have calmed down for now. We waited and watched as the man in the C.S.O. sat with his head hung low. We still had the volume turned on, but nobody was saying anything. As time passed I realized I might have to wait until I come back to find out what would happen. More than likely, if the victim and suspect knew each other it would be called a domestic situation and the man would go to jail.

I was right about having to wait to find out what would happen; before the policeman came to the C.S.O. our relief for dispatch arrived.

"So, that guy's still in the C.S.O., huh," said the officer relieving me. His name was Glen.

"Hiya, Glen." I said happily, "It's been one hell of a night! And yes, Mr. Happy there is still waiting to speak to Metro."

"Anything else to pass on?" Glen asked, "Anything pending?"

"Nah," I answered, "Just the guy in the C.S.O. Pie fights, missing puppets, heart attacks, and ghosts. Rough week, but nothing to really pass on."

"Pie fights?" Glen asked confused.

"Never mind, "I said, "Just normal life in Paradise."

As Matt and I were walking out the door, Glen piped up, "By the way, they found the puppet! It was behind some table; a maid found it while cleaning the room and turned it in."

"Behind a table," I said thoughtfully, thinking about how Hank had grabbed and tossed Mr. Funnybuns across the room the other day, "How lovely! Found it and turned it in!"

"So there's one mystery solved for you guys." Glen said as we continued out the door.

I began to laugh as we walked back to the briefing room. "What's so funny?" Matt asked.

"This place, this job." I answered, still laughing, "This has to be both one of the worst and one of the greatest jobs in the world. Can you imagine doing anything else for a living? Isn't this too much fun to stop?"

Matt gave me a sour look, "You ran off! It was so fun last night you left me in dispatch with a bunch of calls!"

I smiled sheepishly, "Well, I said both the worst and greatest job. I never said there wasn't stress. Besides, I was only gone maybe five minutes!"

We walked in and met up with Paul. He was waiting for us so we could walk to our cars together. "Hello, ladies! Fun night?"

I shook my head, still laughing. "What's so funny?" Paul asked. Hearing the question again just made me laugh harder. Matt went right into the manager's office and found Albert.

"I need a no-lunch swipe!" Matt yelled.

"A no-lunch swipe? Albert asked, "But you guys don't do anything in dispatch! Why would you need a lunch?"

"We don't… you think it's just a picnic?" Matt screamed.

"Calm down," Albert said laughing, "I was just teasing you guys. You did a great job out there last night. I'll give you a no-lunch."

I was swiping out at the time clock as Albert came out. "Wait, wait, wait!" Albert said, "Hold on and I'll use my badge to give you the extra hour for a no-lunch!"

I ignored him and continued to swipe out, "You're a big shot, just change it later." I said.

"Albert stood there with a mad look on his face, "You guys just have to be difficult, don't you?" He asked.

"Yes, we have to be difficult." I repeated as I walked out the door. Out in the hallway Paul and I waited for Matt to get his no-lunch swipe and catch up.

"Hey!" Matt said as he came out the door, "Can't you guys wait a minute?"

"No, we can't just wait a minute." I repeated again. I was feeling really good on the walk out. The start of days off always felt good.

When we got to our cars, Paul said, "See you next week, Robair! You'll be coming back next week, right?"

"What else is there?" I answered, holding my arms out wide, "Goodbye Matthew!" I yelled at his car as he pulled out.

I got in my car and started the engine. Another week down. I wondered to myself what would happen next week, next month, or next year for that matter. It didn't really matter; the future didn't seem so bad. Even with uncooperative officers, lazy people, people who wouldn't answer their radios, this wasn't such a bad job.

After a couple of days off, I'd be back and happy next week.

I did enjoy Paradise Security.

The End
Or is it?

Made in the USA